Dedicated to Elaine Metro,
our friend and colleague

TO THE READER

You are engaged in a challenge of personal, educational, and work competence unlike the challenge extended to any other generation. Your life is far from simple. You know a great deal about yourself and your world. You know what works and what does not work for you. What you do not know, you are willing to discover. You are a person of the twenty-first century.

The purpose of *College and Career Success Simplified* is to take you where you are and to provide an extra "hand up" to your next challenge. No book can succeed for you. But a book organized out of the experiences you and others like you have had will, we believe, give you the extra boost toward success that might otherwise be lacking.

This book offers you ways to integrate the personal, college, and career aspects of your life. What you learn about yourself, about learning, about skills, and about your relationships with others crosses the everyday lines of personal, career, and college considerations.

We know that we learn most effectively by doing. We also know that we learn when we are ready to learn. An ancient Buddhist saying expresses this phenomenon beautifully: "When the student is ready, the teacher will appear." Each of us filters the dynamic of learning differently, based on our experiences, our motivation, and on our unique learning style. We learn both when we succeed and when we fail. We learn more easily when we understand why we need to learn. We learn more easily when we perceive the direct and immediate benefits from what we learn.

College and Career Success Simplified is written out of this awareness. Emphasis is given to simulating your life experiences, out of which learning occurs. We invite you to consider various ways to access your creative and critical thinking power, such as drawing and writing.

We also invite you to be attentive to the process involved in each of the activities in this book—all of which are designed to call forth solutions and applications from personal, work, and college environments. After each activity, we offer you the chance to write your reflections in a journal exercise. You can thus use your response to the activities as a springboard into even greater depths of understanding and meaning.

The integrated activities that follow each section provide you with opportunities to make choices based on what you have learned. Meeting challenges with others is offered as an important alternative to doing everything on your own. This, too, simulates life, where, you will notice, that people working with others in teams makes life easier and more productive.

We have written this book with you in mind. It is designed to help you meet challenges and move on to new frontiers, whatever they may be in your life. We hope you will find our book a friendly print-partner. Because we value your ideas and suggestions, we ask you at the end of this course, to complete the brief questionnaire on page 123.

We are excited by the prospect of your own growing success, and we are privileged to walk with you part of the way. We extend our best wishes to you!

If you would like to contact the authors, please address your email to Harry J. Bury < hbury@bw.edu >.

Harry J. Bury
Susanne M. Alexander
Eileen Teare

George Eppley
Anita Dixon Eppley
Judith Cauley

ABOUT THE AUTHORS

Harry J. Bury Harry J. Bury has taught at Baldwin-Wallace College in Berea, Ohio, since 1979, where he has received many teaching awards, including the Strosaker Award for Excellence in Teaching. He is the Chairman of the Doctorate in Business Administration Program at the Graduate School of Commerce in Burapha University, Bangkok, Thailand. Bury earned his Ph.D. from Case Western Reserve University in Cleveland, Ohio, in 1975. He has been teaching organizational behavior courses in several countries since 1990, including China, Vietnam, Malaysia, and Brazil. Bury also does Organizational Development and Systems Change consulting and cross-cultural training for corporations, healthcare and religious institutions, and government agencies in the U.S. and Asia, such as UMD Pharmaceuticals, TRW, and the United States Federal Reserve Bank.

Susanne M. Alexander Susanne M. Alexander is a full-time freelance journalist specializing in business stories, which have been published in Crain's Cleveland Business and an international edition of Newsweek magazine. She has interviewed executives from companies such as: Microsoft, Avon, Sony, Procter & Gamble, Xerox, McDonald's, and Disney. Alexander has a B.A. in Communications with a business emphasis from Baldwin-Wallace College in Berea, Ohio. She worked for thirteen years at Standard Oil, BP Oil Company, and BP Chemicals as a shipments coordinator, fuel terminal manager, inventory manager, and customer service specialist. She also does copyediting and communications consulting with businesses as president of ClariComm Group. Alexander is co-author of a book on preparation for marriage. Her Website is < **www.claricomm.com** >. She and her husband have four college-age children.

Eileen Teare Eileen Teare is an adjunct English instructor and tutor at Lorain County Community College (LCCC) in Elyria, Ohio, and at Cuyahoga Community College in Parma, Ohio. In 2001 she was nominated by LCCC for the Outstanding Adjunct Teacher Award sponsored by the Ohio Association of Two Year Colleges. She has given tutoring sessions on reading, writing, and study skills and has taught writing skills to employees at the Ford Motor Co. Her prior career was as a high school English teacher. Teare has a B.A. in English from Notre Dame College of Ohio, South Euclid, Ohio, and a Master's in English from John Carroll University, University Heights, Ohio.

George Eppley George Eppley is a professor emeritus of English, Cuyahoga Community College, Cleveland, Ohio, and he has a Ph.D. from Case Western Reserve University in Cleveland. He has been a high school teacher and principal, college professor, graduate school dean, and consultant/innovator for an inner city high school. Dr. Eppley's op-ed pieces have been published in the New York Times, Newsday, and The (Cleveland) Plain Dealer. A frequent guest lecturer and storyteller, his audiotape "Looking Back and Learning" is available in many libraries and bookstores. His Website, The Eppley Files is at < **www.csnmail.net/~eppley/** >. Eppley has co-authored three college composition textbooks with Harcourt Brace, HarperCollins, and Mayfield.

Anita Dixon Eppley Anita Dixon Eppley has taught English composition at Cleveland State University and Cuyahoga Community College in Cleveland, Ohio. She was director of public relations at a Cleveland hospital and has done medical and business freelance writing. Eppley has a Master's degree in English from the University of Notre Dame. She has co-authored three college composition textbooks with Harcourt Brace, HarperCollins, and Mayfield.

Judith Cauley Judith Cauley has a Master's degree in educational administration from St. John College in Cleveland, Ohio, and is a graduate of the Gestalt Institute and the Institute for Spiritual Leadership. She has been a teacher, an innovative school administrator, a superintendent of schools in Colorado Springs, Colorado, an education consultant, and a teacher trainer. Currently, Cauley is associate superintendent of schools for the Archdiocese of Chicago, Illinois.

CHAPTER 1

Using Resources for Success

What is the purpose of a college or university? It is to educate and train, to prepare its student body for the great tasks of life.

—Howard Cosell

To Learn and Understand

- What is networking, and why is it important?
- What resources do you and your college have?
- How can you access them?
- How can they contribute to your success?

1.1 RESOURCES AND NETWORKING

In the work world, asking for help is usually seen as a smart thing to do: "I need you to help me. . .". Such requests are a major secret of success. Asking and seeking assistance as well as being willing to give it builds successful teams both at college and in the workplace. In organizations, **resources** and **resource people** are powerful supports for your success. **Networking**—the power and knowledge gained through associating with others—involves belonging to professional organizations, organizing and working in groups, asking questions, and consulting resource people who are specialists, such as an attorney or an accountant.

People who make themselves aware of resources take their work seriously. They realize how valuable it is to be resourceful in achieving success. Experts agree that most of the opportunity for improvement in business organizations comes from the linkages between people rather than from individuals.

Technical schools, school-to-work academies, community colleges, and four-year colleges are important places to learn networking skills. Utilizing the resources of your school through meeting and learning from the resource experts will provide valuable experience. Through these resources, you can enrich your life, research academic and career topics, and learn skills to make your academic experience more valuable.

Note: *Every college is different in structure, so the following descriptions may not match your college exactly.*

Learning Centers

A *learning center*, sometimes known as a *tutoring center*, assists students who are struggling with particular subject areas. These resources can provide brief assistance sessions or connect a student with a tutor. Some colleges offer special classes or assistance with writing, study skills, or computer basics. The service may provide one-on-one and small-group tutoring in most subjects, as well as workshops and seminars on a variety of topics.

Although a learning center cannot guarantee improvement, most students do experience some degree of added success. Tutors listen to students and help them to understand processes and explore answers. Tutors empower students to find their own answers and to experience their own successes. They also prepare students to seek and utilize **mentors** when they become employees. Mentors teach new employees "the ropes," what they need to know and do to achieve success in their newly chosen careers.

Library/Resource Center

Although you may use the public library in your town or city while you are in college, usually you will use the one on your campus. Campus libraries, sometimes called **resource centers,** have librarians particularly skilled in supporting the needs of college students. They can quickly direct you to Internet, microfilm, and book and publication resources that match your academic needs.

Colleges usually subscribe to various databases or connect with other academic institutions to allow students and faculty greater access to information.

Academic Advising

In most academic settings, counselors or advisors are available to assist you in making wise course choices. They can often assist you in identifying alternative ways to earn credits—for example, through tests, work-study programs, or assessment of prior learning and experience. It is important, therefore, to tell the counselor the timing you have in mind for completing your course of study.

Jacinta Juarez attended community college for a while and earned a few credits. She dropped out and worked for a couple of years before deciding to resume her studies and work toward a four-year computer science degree. She wants to return to the community college for her initial courses and then transfer to a four-year college, but she is unsure about what courses to take, how many credits will transfer, and when to make the transfer.

Jacinta sets up appointments and meets with advisors at both the community college and the university where she wants to complete her degree. They give her course catalogs and clear guidance about transfer credits. She makes careful notes, which she can later refer to each semester as she chooses her courses. Asking for guidance helps her make the best decisions possible.

Career Center

One of your main purposes for attending college is to acquire knowledge that will enable you to have a career when you graduate. Often, however, first-year students do not know what career they want. College career centers provide testing, counseling, and materials to assist the decision-making process. Often they are able to assist with informational interviews, mock interviews, job placement, internships, and resume development.

Staff at the career center can provide information about various careers, which will assist you in choosing courses that move you in the direction of a career that excites and motivates you. If your career will require education at another institution, career centers can provide you with the appropriate information. Make a point to contact them during your first few weeks at college.

1.2 STUDENT ACTIVITIES

Colleges place heavy emphasis on cognitive learning in the classrooms. To be successful, you need to balance this learning with the emotional maturity that comes through building interpersonal skills as well. Many technologically competent people have failed to achieve their career goals because they lacked the desire and the knowledge of how to relate to others. By all means, study. But don't just study—get involved and reach out to others.

Student activities can give you opportunities to establish relationships or to learn skills to support you in career success. They provide you with ways to meet others with similar interests and to learn more about the subjects that interest you. Some clubs or activities in your college may be career-related, such as working on the school newspaper for journalism students. Others may focus on ethnic heritage, religion, the arts, dance, community service, women's issues, or music. Sports activities can range from a spur-of-the-moment game to a formal team, either of which can support fitness and help reduce stress. Often clubs and Greek organizations solicit membership in fall recruiting programs.

Extracurricular activities teach valuable skills, and interaction with others improves interpersonal social skills. Many groups provide opportunities for leadership, organization, record keeping, and teamwork. Noting your involvement on your résumé can make a difference for prospective employers.

Group activities also contribute to a feeling of school spirit and loyalty. They more closely connect students to the operation of the school, and make students better able to represent the school to the public.

Gilberto Camargo was a loner in high school, but he wants to change this in college. Still in his first year, he is unsure what degree to work toward, but he is very interested in the sciences. He glances at the list of campus clubs and spots a biology club that sponsors field trips. Gilberto contacts the club, and they welcome him to join. Their field trips include studying a local wetland area, industrial runoff into a creek, and a preservation project near a bicycle path. He becomes more excited about biology with each trip. By the end of the semester, Gilberto is clear that he wants to be an environmental scientist. He now knows what courses to choose toward achieving this goal.

1.3 BALANCING YOUR NEEDS

All of us have physical, spiritual, emotional, and mental needs. Balancing and using available resources to meet these needs is our responsibility as adults. When we make responsible choices that support us in meeting our needs, we promote our sense of self and improve the quality of our lives. Students often need assistance in understanding and meeting these needs, and you may find it helpful to use the campus health or counseling resources. Counseling is a powerful resource, not a sign of weakness. Your tuition pays for it. Do not be afraid to take advantage of this significant opportunity to grow and be successful in life.

As we change and grow daily, our needs also change. For example, at the physical level, when we were children we needed more sleep than we now need, or we may have gone through growth spurts where we were hungry all the time. Now that we are adults, the amount of sleep and food we need is less, but other needs are more important to us. Perhaps you are a parent, and you have a need for child care. Possibly, you need aerobic exercise in order to think clearly.

On the emotional, mental, and spiritual level, you may recognize a need to think deeply about how you have become the person you are and how you want to grow and change. You may question your parents' beliefs or investigate new religions. Emotionally, you may want to have a significant person or a best friend to enrich your life, or perhaps change something in your personality that is self-defeating, such as depression, prejudice, or being judgmental. Mentally, you may be aware of your need to develop critical-thinking skills to help you solve problems. The balance of these needs changes with the ebb and flow of your life, and your needs frequently blend.

Developing friendships with people who share your need to learn and grow—friends who make studying and attending class a high priority in their lives—is a key to success in college. Networking—for example, finding other students with whom you can study—contributes to success at college. This too is an excellent preparation for later working in teams in the workplace.

Developing relationships with instructors who find joy in helping you learn and grow will enhance your success in college. Being aware of how best you learn (see Chapter 5) and what professors' teaching styles best match your learning style is key to being successful in college.

As a student, you may perceive that the expectations of your school and your professors limit your power of choice and frustration results. While it is true that the academic world has its unique set of expectations—such as going to class, doing homework, and participating in class discussions—so too do families, friends, the government, and employers, all of whom test your inner strength. Those external expectations need not deplete your own sense of personal power, however. Strength comes from making your own choices within the framework in which you are living and working.

Wu Qin Ya's professor informed her that if she did not turn in a required paper, she might fail the class. Her professor's comment prompted her to look at her decisions regarding the class. First, she realized that she was not a morning person, yet she had signed up for an 8 A.M. class three days a week. She was taking two classes, totaling eight credit hours, working twenty hours a week, and serving on the student council. Wu Qin Ya realized that she was not acting in her own best interest. She needed to examine her life, her priorities, her goals, and her limitations. Consider what you might do in similar circumstances.

You have the right to access resources to meet your needs, both at school and at work. Often this requires a higher level of assertiveness than you may be accustomed to. In her book *Assertiveness Training*, Betsy N. Callahan suggests that everyone has the following rights:

1. You have the right and the responsibility to control your own life.
2. You have the right to hold and express your own feelings, thoughts, and opinions, and to be your own judge.
3. You have the right to be treated with respect and to be taken seriously.
4. You have the right to err and to change your mind.
5. You have the right to be human (not perfect) and not to be liked by everyone.
6. You have the right to make and refuse requests without feeling guilty.
7. You have the right to get what you pay for.
8. You have the right to choose not to pursue a personal right.

Each of us has the opportunity to determine our own needs and how to meet them. Rarely are we alone in these activities, however. It is important to find the resources we need, to ask for assistance, and not just try to cope on our own. Asking for help is an action of strength, not weakness. As we continue to awaken to our rights and responsibilities, we will come to know what we need to know, and grow as we need to grow.

■ TIPS FOR SUCCESS ■
Resources, Activities, and Needs

1. Recognize when you need academic assistance, and request it before you get into serious trouble.
2. Become familiar with the library before you urgently need information for an assignment.
3. Ask for assistance from librarians, and express gratitude.
4. Explore the academic advising and career resources early in your college experience.
5. Carefully evaluate all your options for extracurricular activities, and choose a small number that match your interests and enhance rather than interfere with your academics.
6. Form a study group with excellent students who are taking the same courses as you are.
7. Keep a daily journal to record your reflections and feelings. (Note how it is almost impossible to write in a journal without, at the same time, living an authentic life—endeavoring to be the same person inside that you present to the world.)
8. Associate with successful people who respect and encourage you.
9. Commit to regular aerobic exercising, fitness training, and participating in sports.

SCENARIO FOR SUCCESS

At the end of the third week of her first year at college, Clarissa Amirette felt overwhelmed. She had three term papers to work on, and she was struggling with her writing. She knew she had to ask for help.

Clarissa's first stop was at the Resource Center/Library. She asked the librarian for a quick overview of the facility and then shared with him the subjects of her term papers. He spent ten minutes with her helping her outline the key materials she would need for each assignment and where to find them.

The second stop was the Writing Lab, where she was able to set up a series of appointments with a tutor for assistance. The tutor agreed to review her drafts of the term papers and give her guidance on grammar, punctuation, and sentence structure.

For the first time in three weeks, Clarissa discovered she could breathe again. Her tension dissipated, and she finally could relax. Confidence in herself grew as she experienced the college's resources supporting her needs.

Questions for Discussion
1. How did you manage a situation in your life that was similar to Clarissa's?
2. What are the warning signs that you might need to ask for assistance?
3. How would you know what assistance to ask for?
4. What do you need to prepare before approaching someone to ask for assistance?
5. When you ask for assistance, what are the responsibilities of your resource person, and what are yours?

ACTIVITIES FOR SUCCESS

Activity 1: Researching College Resources

The school you attend has a variety of centers and offices that can help you in the decisions you need to make and the projects you will be completing throughout your college career.

Objective: To become familiar with the resources of the college.
Procedure:
    Step 1: The teacher will divide the class into small groups and assign one campus resource center to each group to investigate.
    Step 2: Each team presents to the class a brief report on one of the resource centers. Include the following information: location; hours open; contact person; key features; benefits of using; any other information that would be valuable for students to know.

Activity 2: Researching Work Resources

At your workplace, another effective way to be successful is to understand your own section and how it fits into the entire organization.

Objective: To become familiar with the resources of your workplace.

Procedure:

Step 1: Tour the company. After touring it, research the organization's mission statement and the strategic objectives in place for achieving the mission. Interview a manager to receive an individual perspective on how better the organization can achieve its mission. Begin to picture yourself fitting into the organization as a vital contributor to the mission.

Step 2: Present your findings to the class.

JOURNAL FOR SUCCESS

Journal Entry 1

Objective: To become more aware of how your resources enable you to be successful.

Procedure: List the school and/or work resources you are already familiar with and indicate how these resources have enabled you to be more successful.

Journal Entry 2

Objective: To increase awareness of your assertiveness.

Procedure: Reflect on and write about Betsy N. Callahan's eight rights and your experience with them (see page 3). Where do you see room for improvement in being more assertive in your quest for success?

CHAPTER 2

Using the Computer for Success

*Imagination has brought mankind through the Dark Ages to its present state of civilization. **Imagination** led Columbus to discover America. **Imagination** led Franklin to discover electricity. **Imagination** has given us the steam engine, the telephone, the talking-machine, and the automobile, for these things had to be dreamed before they became realities.*

—L. Frank Baum

To Learn and Understand

- What are the benefits of staying current with computer software?
- What methods can you use to stay current?
- How can you use computers responsibly?
- How can you keep your computer running smoothly?

2.1 STAYING CURRENT WITH COMPUTERS

One of the biggest benefits to us today is the rapid expansion of information and communication technology, with computers, faxes, the Internet, cellular phones, and the like becoming necessities. Students at universities and new employees in organizations are expected to understand and use these new areas of discovery. Technology changes so rapidly, however, that a top-of-the-line computer purchased today will be considered old news a few months from now. So what can *you* do?

Stay current.

Colleges are now using technology as a prime selling feature to prospective students. With student e-mail accounts, campus-wide access to the Internet, free computer support, and workshops, most students have easy access to learning about technology and incorporating it into their personal lives in college.

Most employers utilize computers in the workplace—which means that without some computer skills, it is difficult to be hired at many companies. To keep employees current, companies often schedule on-site training seminars for their employees, or they provide funding for computer classes or access to books and software to learn programs at home. Employers recognize that it is critical to the success of their businesses to have employees who are up-to-date on technology.

It is in your best interest to take advantage of all such learning opportunities. Make it a personal priority to brush up on your keyboarding/typing skills or learn a new software program. Have fun with technology. Learning new skills gives you a sense of accomplishment in organizing your personal life and helps you become more successful in today's fast-paced society.

Methods for Learning New Technology

The following suggestions will get your computer use and learning off to a good start.

Accessing Computers   Most of you became familiar with basic computer skills long before college. Now, however, you will probably need to know more software programs and functions to be successful. Visit your college's computer service center to inquire about the technology options available for students on campus. If you own a computer and want to bring it with you to college, find out the requirements for setting up and connecting a computer in the residence halls or common areas. You might also want to check with your roommates to see if they too have computers and are willing to share them. Check with the university to find out the ways to get onto the university network. As soon as possible, familiarize yourself with the computer labs on campus. Note where they are located in proximity to your dorm or classroom, the hours they are open, and whom to contact if you have questions.

Saving Your Work   Saving documents as you work on your computer is important. Many students have horror stories of working on a term paper or project all night long, only to have it lost during a brief power failure or a computer shutdown. It is best to save your document at least every ten minutes and to make at least one backup copy of it on a diskette or CD. Many software programs have a setting that will automatically back up a document, so use this, but don't count on it. Technology is great, but it is not foolproof. Often a company will have a network that has a backup copy of everything employees create. If you lose a document, a technology professional may be able to help you recover it.

Understanding System Utilities   One benefit of becoming familiar with system utilities is knowing how much space is available on the drives and knowing how to **defragment** the drives occasionally to keep them running faster and help eliminate system crashes. In the process of **defragging**, the operating system (OS) reconfigures data to make the computer run more efficiently and to optimize the hard disk space. Computer capabilities are dependent on available disk space. If you load large programs such as computer games onto a computer drive with limited space, system crashes are inevitable.

Setting Up an E-mail Account   Some colleges set up e-mail accounts for students before they arrive. Check with the computer help center (or similar office) to find out how to create your password and/or log on to your e-mail account and the Internet. Once you have this set up, make sure you have your account name and password written down in a secure place, and do not share it with anyone. Besides, forgetting it and not being able to get to important documents is a hassle you can easily do without. To protect your privacy, the computer center probably will not have access to this information.

Consulting with Professors   Professors can be a great source of information about computers, especially if you have an assignment due to be created on an unfamiliar computer program. Empowered with the networking skills you learned in Chapter 1, make an appointment with your professor to ask for tips about using the program, and give yourself plenty of time to work on the project. That way, if you encounter any glitches, you can take care of the problem without jeopardizing your project. Also, at the computer help desk (or similar office), student proctors and full-time employees are on hand much of the time to answer questions, and they can walk you through a process while you are at the computer.

Enrolling in Technical Courses   Many career centers, continuing education offices, community centers, and community colleges, among others, also have classes on technology. The topics can range from the fundamentals of keyboarding to accessing the Internet or using a publishing program to make your own Website. You can also find courses offered at your local library, another good place for computer access.

Purchasing Needed Software   If you prefer to learn on your own, purchase a copy of a software program. Compare prices at your campus bookstore, nearby computer centers, and Internet sites. The benefit of having this software on hand is that you can set up your own system for learning and do it at your own pace. Set a time-line for yourself that you are comfortable following. If you learn a software program and see how it can benefit you in your schoolwork, you will be comfortable using it in the workplace.

Be aware that sharing software among a variety of users can be illegal. Software needs to be licensed to a particular user or company.

2.2 USING THE INTERNET

The Internet is expanding at such an exponential rate that phone companies are creating new area codes, phone numbers, and access methods to keep up with the increasing number of people using it. Through the Internet, people can research information and connect with each other from virtually anywhere in the world 24 hours a day, 7 days a week. Unlimited communications and broadcasting possibilities are available with just a couple of clicks of a computer mouse button.

How to Access the Internet

You can reach the Internet through **Internet Service Providers (ISPs).** With so many being created, it is hard to keep an up-to-date, comprehensive list, but two examples you might be familiar with are America Online (AOL) and Microsoft Network (MSN). These ISPs give you the means to access diverse information source sites—from pet breeding to genealogy research to vacation planning. Generally, you need to pay for the access if you are on your home computer, where many students prefer to do their research.

Some ISPs, however, are free. (Note that you should have free access to an ISP through your college's network. Check with the technology department for specific information regarding your school's connectivity.) If you wish to access a free ISP, you need to be careful. Some free suppliers limit your access time and may only be available through local telephone service to a limited geographical area. Paying long-distance telephone charges each time you access an ISP can be costly. In addition, the advertising on free ISPs can be overwhelming, and their help/support services may be lacking in quality. In other words, you get what you pay for. Check around to find the terms and limitations of different providers and decide which one is the best fit for you. Some things to consider are how much you can afford to spend per month on Internet access, how much time you will be spending on the Internet, and what capabilities you want. Some ISPs provide access to the Internet and give you an e-mail account, while others give you Internet access only or e-mail access only.

How to Find Information on the Internet

To locate information through the Internet, you will use what is called a **search engine**—a tool that searches multiple Websites at once. Search engines are commonly used on the **World Wide Web (www)** to retrieve information on a specific topic, theme, name, and so forth. By keying in words that identify your search or by entering a **query,** you can define the parameters of a search. The search engine matches your query with available sites and lists them. Some search engines give better sets of search results than others and place the most important information at the top of the results list. You will choose your favorites over time with experience.

Here are some examples of the most popular search engines:

yahoo.com	overture.com
google.com	infoseek.com
askjeeves.com	msn.com
dogpile.com	lycos.com
altavista.com	hotbot.com

You can search the Internet in much the same way you would look for something in the library, either by typing in some key words describing what you are seeking or typing in an exact title of what you want. For example, if you are looking for information on a book and you know only the author's name, you can type it in and look for information relating to that author. Search engines also enable you to narrow or expand your search.

SEARCHING THE INTERNET

- Type in the keyword (can be single or multiple words).
- View the list of Websites ("hits").
- Click on the Website you would like to view.
- Look at the hyperlinks on the Website that you view. Often a site will link to other sites containing related information.

If you find a Website you want to revisit later, most Internet providers give you the capability of marking it with a "bookmark" or "favorite places" function. The next time you want to go there, you can just click directly on your personal bookmark.

Internet Search Example

Using < **www.msn.com** > to search the Web for Freiburg, a German city located in the foothills of the Black Forest, one can find a results list of various sites. These include links to the University of Freiburg; the University's Drosophila Lab, which conducts research into the development of a fly's brain; La Gamba Freiburg, a specialist ensemble that performs Baroque and pre-Baroque chamber music for violas da gamba; and the city of Freiburg's official Website (see Figure 2.1 on pages 10–11).

If you conducted a similar search today, you would probably find a different results list because sites have new information, new sites are created, and sites are discontinued. After a quick glance at the list of sites, you can go to the Websites that seem likely to have the information that is relevant to your research.

Evaluating Internet Information

The Internet is a rapidly expanding medium on which people are establishing Websites very quickly. Many are not kept current with revisions. So, a word of caution is in order before you use Suzy's aromatherapy Website as a formal reference in your anatomy and physiology paper about different treatments for muscle pain. You need to know the information you are referencing is legitimate.

Determining Page Authorship   "You can tell a lot about the authenticity of a Website by finding out all you can about its author/publisher," says Gary Griffith, a computer instructor at Polaris Career Center in Cleveland. "Ask yourself this," he advises. "Who is responsible for the site you are accessing? Is it a governmental agency or other official source? A university? A business, corporation, or other commercial interest? An individual? As a rule of thumb, you can generally rely on the GOV and EDU hostnames to present accurate information. The NET, ORG, MIL, and COM domains are more likely to host sites with their own personal or organizational agendas and might require additional verification."

Checking the Content   Any individual on the Web can be his or her own publisher, and many are. "Don't accept everything you read just because it's printed on a Website," warns Griffith. "Unlike scholarly books and journal articles," he says, "Websites are seldom reviewed or refereed. It's up to you to check for bias and to determine objectivity." Who sponsors the site? Who is linking to the site? What links to other sites does the site itself maintain? Is there an e-mail link for questions and comments and the name, address, telephone number, and e-mail address of the site owner?

Look to see if the page owner tells you when the page was last updated. Is the information current? Can it be verified at other, similar sites? Try to distinguish between promotion, advertising, and serious content. This is getting to be more difficult, as an increasing number of sites must look to commercial support for their continuance.

In many cases, you can e-mail the webmasters responsible for maintaining Websites to inquire about their sources of information. Some Websites post official statements acknowledging or disclaiming affiliation with or support from an organization.

Information on a government-sponsored site such as that of the National Institutes of Health < **www.nih.gov** >, is likely to be more factual and unbiased than information on a company-sponsored site that has a product to sell. Generally, sites that are designed to market company products and services present only their most positive image. You can find a more unbiased approach at a site such as < **www.hoovers.com** >, which was created to provide objective information about businesses.

You can check the reliability of Internet sources by using a growing number of Websites dedicated to evaluating sources. One example is < **www.wilkes.edu/library/stories/storyReader$29** > offered by Wilkes University. Use a search engine to find other sites that can help you evaluate Internet sources. If you are in doubt about the accuracy or reliability of information on a Website, however, your college or city librarians can suggest ways to evaluate it.

Watch out for deliberate frauds and hoaxes. Some people really enjoy making mischief on the Web. You can check these out at < **www.snopes.com** > or < **www.symantec.com/avcenter/hoax.html** >.

Assessing Website Stability   There is no way to freeze a Website in time. Unlike the print world with its publication dates, editions, ISBN numbers, and so forth, Websites are fluid. There is no bibliographic control on the Web. The page you cite today may be altered or revised tomorrow, or it may disappear completely. The site owner may or may not acknowledge the changes, and if the page is relocated, the owner may or may not leave a forwarding address or a link to which you can connect.

Try to assess the stability of the sites you reference. Again, one of the best ways to do this is to look closely at the site sponsor, when the site was last updated, and the credibility of the Website owners.

When you are writing a paper and using Websites as source material, keep a backup of what you find on the Web (either as a printout or saved to disk, diskette, or CD), so that you can verify your sources later if need be.

Protecting Your Data from Viruses   Unfortunately, there are computer users who create **viruses**—unauthorized programs that can enter your computer and "infect" it. A virus can be in an e-mail, a document attached to an e-mail, or in an instant message. Viruses can corrupt data on your computer, cause your hard drive to fail, or send automatic and infected messages to people in your e-mail address book. Organizations and individual computer users can protect their computers with **antivirus software.** This software must be updated continually (usually at least weekly) to stop new viruses.

2.3 PERSONAL BENEFITS OF USING THE INTERNET

Using the Internet gives you access to a great deal of information you need for academic research and for your personal growth. It can save you trips to the bookstore and the library. Stores that offer online catalogs of their merchandise give you the opportunity to shop from home. You can also search the Internet for competitively priced airline tickets, which makes trips home on breaks more affordable. Banks offer online bill-paying services and loan/credit applications. Children can access learning centers created just for children, and college students, no matter what their age or academic discipline, can access libraries around the world or around the block from home in seconds.

A word of caution: One of the unfortunate aspects of the growth of the Internet is that many sites feature pornography or what some would consider questionable material. Be cautious about going into sites that might contain explicit material, especially if there are children nearby. Many employers are now using software that tracks the amount of time employees spend on the Internet and what sites they visit. Employees have been fired for visiting non-work-related sites and for spending excessive amounts of time online for personal use. Others have been arrested for downloading illegal material to corporate computers.

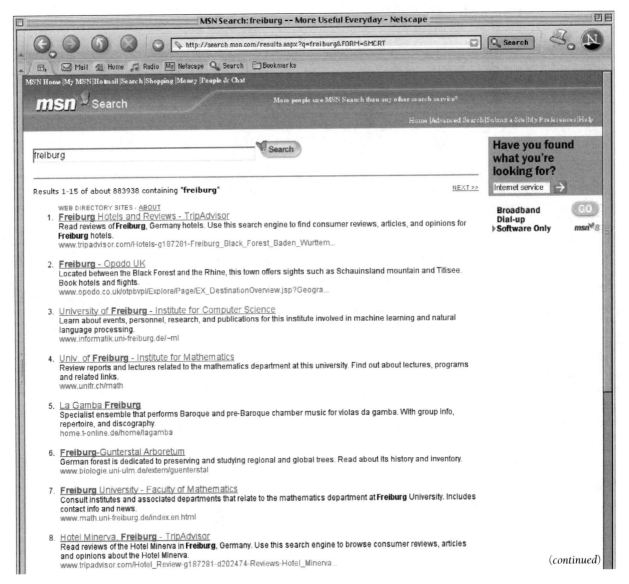

Figure 2.1 ■ Example of a list of hyperlinks to Websites that a search engine has identified as relevant to search.

2.4 E-MAIL ETIQUETTE

Many companies, schools, and organizations have internal e-mail capabilities (often called an Intranet), and most companies have the ability to send e-mail to outside parties. Many teachers use e-mail for assignments or to answer students' questions. One of the most attractive features of e-mail is how quickly and how widely it is possible to send messages. This can also be a hazard, however, and all users should be aware of the rules of e-mail etiquette.

Watching Your Tone and Content   Creating and sending a message with an angry tone—what is called **flaming**—can have a negative impact. People have lost relationships and even their jobs because they didn't pause to cool off before sending a message. As with any form of communication, think of the message you want to send, and put it in the first person to lessen any sense of accusation or blame ("This is how I felt when I found I was being taken off the team due to personality problems"). Remember that people cannot see your facial expressions along with messages, so be certain your reader will clearly understand when you are joking and when you are serious. Messages sent in ALL CAPS should be avoided because they communicate that you are shouting. Ha, Ha or LOL (laughing out loud) at the end of a sentence indicates you are joking.

Remember that it is almost impossible to delete or retrieve a message once it is sent. Make sure the content is not embarrassing and that it does not contain something you might later regret. Ask yourself if the message could be a problem in the hands of someone other than the intended recipient. Messages can easily be forwarded or

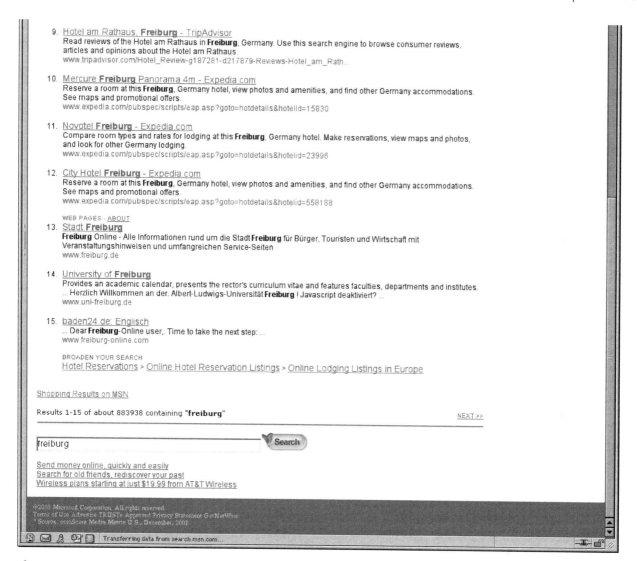

Figure 2.1 (*continued*)

accidentally sent to the wrong address. Electronic copies of e-mails are often kept in the computer systems of organizations or companies, so consider whether there could be a problem if your message is kept indefinitely. E-mail sent from a company computer is not your personal property, but in fact belongs to the company and can be admissible in a court of law.

Manners Count   Although e-mail is quick and easy, take the extra second to add a salutation and end with *Sincerely*, or whatever you would use when writing or typing any other correspondence. Include your whole name at the end, especially if your e-mail address does not identify you. (Since many people often know more than one Barbara, for instance, a last name will help to avoid confusion.) When appropriate, you should also include your title and the organization you represent. Because the personal element of face-to-face presence is lost in e-mail communication, it is important to take extra care to be polite and complete in your communications. Another point of courtesy is asking permission to forward to someone else a message that the sender addressed to you.

Being Accurate   Although grammar, spelling, and punctuation errors are more easily forgiven on e-mail, it's still important to remember that whatever you write represents you and/or your organization, so proofread e-mail before sending it and run a spelling check if your software has that capability. This is especially important if the message is going externally to a customer or supplier or to a professor responsible for grading your work. Apply to e-mail the same standards for accuracy and courtesy you would use in writing hard-copy documents.

Being Clear and Concise   Because many people often receive a large number of e-mail messages, it is helpful if you clearly identify the topic of your message in the subject line so a receiver can judge whether it requires urgent attention. The body of the message then needs to be as clear and concise as possible so it can be read or scanned quickly. More and more people are becoming irritated with forwarded jokes and stories. Make sure your message really needs to be sent.

Checking Company Policy on Personal Messages   Many companies have policies about sending personal e-mail during work hours. Some offer the opportunity to send personal e-mail on lunch breaks or after work hours, and some prohibit personal e-mail of any kind. Check with your supervisor, human resources department, or information technology personnel about what is and what is not acceptable. Few employers are willing to allow employees to use what could be productive work time on nonwork items.

2.5 PERSONAL BENEFITS OF E-MAIL

E-mail is a great way to communicate because of its speed, efficiency, and low cost. There is no stationery to purchase, and there are no stamps to buy, no post offices to visit, and no pens to run out of ink. Keeping in touch with relatives, friends, or business associates who live at a distance can be much easier with e-mail. Plus, many people prefer e-mail correspondence because it is right in front of them and does not get lost in a pile of papers on the desk.

You can also send the same message to multiple individuals, saving an immense amount of time. Moreover, such messages increase the communication factor in an organization (and eliminate excuses and complaints about poor communication). If you are sensitive to the need others have for information, you can utilize this technology to inform many colleagues at once. If you err, err on the side of too much information and no secrets. Those who do not need the information can easily hit the delete key.

Listserves

Another benefit of e-mail and the Internet are **listserves**—group e-mail distribution mechanisms that enable everyone on an electronic mailing list to receive every message posted by members for discussion. By using listserves, a group of individuals who are interested in the same topic can interact through e-mail communication. Members can trade stories, share knowledge and experience, ask questions, and seek advice or give advice about different topics. Some professors have put an entire class on a listserve to foster increased communication and networking. You can use a search engine to search for the word "LISTSERV", or "listserve", to find lists to join.

Listserves enable people to reply to an individual who sends a message or to everyone on the list. If you aren't careful when replying to an e-mail, however, you might send a message intended for an individual to the whole group. This could have serious repercussions. To make sure you are using the listserve correctly, check the user guidelines. Some discussion listserves are free, and some require a nominal fee for membership.

2.6 OWNERSHIP OF INFORMATION

The general rule regarding ownership of information has to do with where the information is located. If it is on your own computer hard drive, you own that information (not the programs, which you just license). If your information is on your employer's computer or network, the employer owns it. Employees sometimes refer to the computers they use as "theirs," but in fact those computers are simply provided to them temporarily to do their work.

2.7 USING SOFTWARE SUITES

The most common software in schools and offices is the software suite—a set of application programs offered by several different companies. Lotus has its Lotus SmartSuite, and Microsoft has its Microsoft Office, one of the most popular suite packages on the market today. The Microsoft Office software covers most of the duties performed in an office—writing, making a presentation slide show, calculating and analyzing financial affairs, and managing databases. Some of the programs commonly found in a Microsoft Office package include Word (for word processing), Excel (for spreadsheets), Access (for databases), PowerPoint (for presentations), and Outlook (for calendar, contacts, and e-mail). When selecting a software package, be aware that some are much more commonly used than others, and using them might make interfacing with other users easier and more reliable. It's a good idea to invest in software programs that are compatible with those used by your instructors, your workplace, and others with whom you communicate regularly.

2.8 SAVING ENERGY AND MONEY

Set your personal computer (PC) to go to a power save mode after about thirty minutes of inactivity, so it will hibernate while you are not using it. Be sure to shut it down altogether when you do not expect to use it for a long period of time. Taking these precautions will conserve electric power, and you, your college, and your company will benefit by reduced electric bills. Setting up a **screensaver** to appear on your screen after a few minutes of no activity will preserve the clarity of the screen on your monitor.

> ### ■ TIPS FOR SUCCESS ■
> #### Computer Usage
>
> 1. When learning a new process or program, go to the help pages. Print them out if necessary, and make notes. Keep a personal log of exactly what you had to do to create a document and perform key functions. Then, when you need to do it again, you will have your own self-help manual at hand.
> 2. If you think you will need an important document for later reference, print it out or back it up on a diskette or CD. Data backup is extremely important but often overlooked. When you consider backup solutions, provide for backup media comparable in size to the information you have stored on your regular disk drive. For backing up larger quantities of data, consider using tape backup or an Internet backup service.
> 3. When doing research, check any information you find on the Internet to make sure that it is accurate and up-to-date.
> 4. When using an e-mail service, remember that everything you write reflects upon you as a person. Hence, make every effort to be courteous, and check content for correct grammar and spelling.
> 5. Set the computer on a power save mode to maximize the life of the hardware and save energy as well as needless expense. Be sure to turn the computer off at the end of the day.

SCENARIO FOR SUCCESS

Maria Montaya is a freshman at Hill University. Although she has used a computer, she was largely unaware of the different types of software programs available, and she has rarely used the Internet for serious research. After her first day of classes, she and her roommate went to the computer service center and signed up for workshops on word processing programs and Internet use. Maria learned how to access and search the Internet for information for her coursework, and she used her research and newfound knowledge about word processing for her freshman English term paper on Langston Hughes. She received an excellent grade on her paper and felt more confident about her research abilities.

Questions for Discussion

1. What would you like to learn about using the Internet?
2. Have you taken advantage of your school's technology resources the way Maria did, and if so, what was the result?
3. What other ways can you increase your technology skills to increase your opportunities for success in school?
4. Have you used a computer in the workplace? How did it enable you to be more effective?

ACTIVITIES FOR SUCCESS

Activity 1: Becoming Familiar with a Software Program

You might be unfamiliar with some computer functions that could make your job much easier. It is to your advantage to learn how to use these functions.

Objectives: (1) To expand your knowledge of how to use a computer; (2) to learn how to design and use a step-by-step plan of action.

Procedure:

Step 1: Write down five tasks that you would like to learn how to do or how to do better on a computer, in order of your highest preference first to your lowest.

Step 2: Take the first one and set a timeline for yourself showing the steps you can take to learn about it. Make sure that your timeline is realistic yet personally challenging.

Step 3: Write down what benefits you will have in your life by learning this. Now do the same steps for the other four tasks.

Step 4: Take the steps that you listed in Step 2 and actually do them, keeping your timeline in mind.

Step 5: Repeat Steps 2 through 4 for the other four tasks you would like to learn how to do or how to do better.

Activity 2: Using and Evaluating Search Engines

At the first meeting of the semester of a campus community service club, members discuss what project to adopt for the semester. The group decides they want to help a group of refugees in their town who are from a country in central Africa (e.g., Burundi, Rwanda, Cameroon, or Chad). The students immediately recognize, however, that they don't know anything about the language, culture, food, or customs of the people with whom they want to interact. As a member of the club, you volunteer to be on a committee to search the Internet for details, print them out, and bring them back to the group for discussion.

Objectives: (1) To practice using search engines for research; (2) to evaluate several search engines, comparing their ease of use, the quality of information they provide, and any other features you discover as you conduct your research.

Procedure: Work in small groups.

Step 1: Select a country to research. Assign one of the following topics to each member of your group: (1) language, (2) culture, (3) food, or (4) customs.

Step 2: Select a search engine to conduct your research—one you are familiar with or one you have not used in the past. You might want to select one of those listed earlier in this chapter (in Section 2.2 Using the Internet).

Step 3: Conduct your research, print out your results, and report back to the group.

Step 4: As a class, compare and rate the search engines you used according to the ease of finding information and the quality of the information.

Activity 3: Evaluating and Handling Virus Warnings

If you frequently send and receive e-mail, you probably get messages from time to time from well-meaning friends who forward messages containing dire warnings about new viruses. Evaluating virus warnings and dealing responsibly with them is important in protecting your own computer as well as the computers of those with whom you communicate by e-mail.

Objectives: (1) To learn what antivirus programs are available; (2) to compare the features and prices of at least two antivirus programs.

Procedure: Work in small groups.

Step 1: Together, conduct an Internet search for antivirus programs.

Step 2: Alone or with a partner, find information about the features and cost of several programs.

Step 3: Compare your findings with one another, and decide which program best fits your needs.

JOURNAL FOR SUCCESS

Journal Entry 1

Objective: To become more aware of how successful you can be when you push your **comfort zone**, do something you find challenging, let go of your fears, and actively try to learn new things on the computer.

Procedure: Evaluate how successful you were with accomplishing your computer learning goals in a timely manner in Activity 1. Note how helpful these new skills will be to you in the future. Write about your feelings while attempting to learn these new skills.

CHAPTER 3
Success in Managing Time

Just for today I will have a program. I may not follow it exactly, but I will have it. I will save myself from two pests: hurry and indecision.

—Al-Anon Family Groups

To Learn and Understand

- What practical methods assist you in managing time?
- What are the characteristics of people who manage time well?
- How does planning your time help you to accomplish goals?
- How do values relate to time management?

3.1 IMPORTANCE OF TIME MANAGEMENT

Are you often late for appointments? Do you misplace or lose things frequently? Do you complain that you do not have enough time to do what you need and want to do? Are you frustrated? Often exhausted? Do you misjudge how much time it takes to get from one place to another? Do you procrastinate when you have a deadline to meet? The night before a test do you watch the late, late movie? Do you organize your chest of drawers when you need to be writing a paper for class? Does it take an extraordinary length of time for you to get started on a project? Does time just seem to sneak up on you and take you by surprise?

You can probably answer "yes" to one or more of the above questions. However, you have also probably said at one time or another, "Time just flew by" or, when you were involved in some creative project, "I lost all track of time." From your experience, then, you know that there are times when you do manage time rather than time managing you. If you were able to change your perception of the limitations of time, you would be able to manage time more expeditiously and fruitfully.

Deepak Chopra explores characteristics of timeless awareness in his book *Ageless Body, Timeless Mind.* He identifies the following characteristics of creative people who manage time well:

- Satisfaction that one is doing one's best
- Sense that time is abundant and open-ended
- Little thought of self-image
- Reliance on intuition and leaps of imagination
- Detachment from change and turmoil
- Positive experiences of well-being
- Selflessness; a willingness to use time to help others

3.2 PLANNING AHEAD

Key parts of time management are **planning** and **goal setting**. Planning enables you to accomplish whatever personal, career, or academic goals you have set for yourself. Planning keeps you on top of things and gets you organized. When you have planned your time well, you feel in control of your life. This reduces stress and helps you to evaluate your priorities.

With your time planned, you will find that you are able to keep on schedule more easily. When unexpected things happen, you can more easily adjust. You can allow "free" time for yourself. Such time promotes creativity and opportunities to be with other people, both of which are fulfilling and rewarding. You even find time to rest, which results in more energy and productivity when you return to your studies. Planning helps to maximize your efficiency. Most importantly, planning promotes a balanced approach to living (see Chapter 16) and ensures that life runs somewhat smoothly.

Shim Nozei is having trouble turning in his assignments on time. Every night, friends drop by his house and want to play music and video games. He doesn't want to be rude, so each time, he plays with them and doesn't do his homework. Unhappy with his grades, however, he realizes he has to take control of planning his time. He chooses two days and times each week as "free" time, and he lets his friends know that he isn't available at other times. They are disappointed, but they soon learn to respect his determination to do well in school.

3.3 USING A DAILY PLANNER

Managing time is easier when you use a daily planner and write out your objectives for each day. Most people use a date book to record appointments. A person who wants to manage time effectively will also record project deadlines or other action steps to be taken to achieve goals.

It is helpful to use a daily planner that is organized by the hour or in morning, afternoon, and evening sections. When you have a project due, enter the date due in the planner. Then, working backward, set short-term objectives for accomplishing the project. By using scheduling techniques along with your own sense of timing, you can manage time more effectively and successfully control your life more efficiently.

In the workplace, many people prefer to use a **Personal Digital Assistant (PDA)**, an electronic device for managing time successfully. It is so beneficial that many companies will buy this device for their employees. The popular Palm Pilot is an example. Many PDAs can be connected to your personal computer through a "cradle" device, which enables you to back up your information and easily enter new information. The connection to the cradle also enables you to share certain information with other PDA users. With these devices you can keep a calendar, an extensive address book, "to do" lists, and expense records, and do various kinds of note taking and many other activities. A PDA will even enable you to go onto the Internet for e-mail and other purposes from just about any location.

Note: *The activities at the end of this chapter will provide you with an opportunity to understand and practice planning a daily schedule.*

3.4 IDENTIFYING YOUR VALUES

It is important to understand that you allocate your time based on what is important to you. If you value enjoying nature more than an organized house, you might choose to go for a walk rather than organize your closets. If you value your relationship with friends more than cooking a gourmet meal, you might arrange to spend time with a friend at a restaurant instead of shopping and cooking for hours. Each event or task that you put into your daily planner needs to be balanced against your identified values. A note of caution: If you value high grades and the knowledge they represent, you may need to courageously say "no" when classmates urge you to quit studying and go out with them for some fun activity.

■ TIPS FOR SUCCESS ■
Time Management

1. Plan ahead.
2. Concentrate on one thing at a time.
3. Simplify your life and your schedule as much as possible.
4. Recognize and honor your limitations.
5. Maintain balance in your time choices between mind, body, and spirit.
6. Learn when to say "no."
7. Learn when to say "yes."
8. Go with the flow.
9. Block out stray thoughts from the matter at hand.
10. Allow yourself to deal with the matter at hand easily, without intensity, but with concentration.
11. Be patient with yourself if your attention span is low. With practice, it will improve.

SCENARIO FOR SUCCESS

Elaya Montaabi, a senior in college, was really pressed for time. She always seemed to be running from one place to the next without any time to slow down. She was frequently late to her job at the dining hall, and sometimes she would forget to meet her housemates for dinner or forget an appointment with her study group. She was constantly stressed out and nervous as a result. For a birthday present, her parents sent her some money and told her to get what she needed. Elaya went to the campus bookstore and bought herself a daily planner (which was going to be helpful in scheduling postgraduate job interviews, too). She sat down that night and penciled in all of her class assignments from the syllabus for each class. She also scheduled her work hours and her breaks for the week. Soon she was entering new appointments, meetings, and other items—such as what nights she was responsible for cooking dinner. Elaya soon stopped missing appointments, and her anxiety level dropped dramatically.

Questions for Discussion

1. Are you, like Elaya, finding yourself pressed for time? Describe what life is like as a result.
2. Which tips for success have you found personally helpful in your efforts to manage your time successfully?
3. What other techniques could you suggest to the class that have worked for you in managing your time?

ACTIVITIES FOR SUCCESS

Activity 1: Weekly Planning—Perception Versus Reality

Often you may not have a clear understanding of what you actually do with your time. This exercise will help you understand what you think you do with it and what actually happens.

Objectives: (1) Record your perceived schedule; (2) record your actual schedule.

Procedure: On a piece of paper, write down your schedule for each day as you know it, using a format like the one shown in Figure 3.1 (see page 18). Then, as the week progresses, write down how much time each activity actually took, using the schedule shown in Figure 3.2 (see page 19). At the end of the second week, compare your two schedules and adjust accordingly. This will give you a better idea of what needs more time and where you can let up a bit.

   Make a note of any observations you have about your difference in scheduling demands as evidenced by this new schedule.

Activity 2: Time Management

Excellent time management requires that you spend your time according to your values. Knowing what these values are helps you allocate your time.

Objectives: (1) Identify your core values; (2) match your values with activity choices; (3) understand how to allocate your time; (4) practice planning a daily schedule.

Procedure:

   Step 1: Look at the following list of values and time choices. Choose the ones that apply to you, and add any others that are important to you.

Lifelong learning	Playing games	Artistic activities
Obtaining a college degree	Financial security	Exercising
Teaching or mentoring others	Ethnic activities	Dining out/cooking
Creativity	Neatness	High grades
Family/children	Community service	Setting goals
Beauty of nature	Friendships	Meditation
Risk-taking sports	Appearance	Homework/studying
Sports for fun	Music	Leadership activities/clubs
Religious activities/prayer	Dancing	Computer/Internet activities

Time	Sunday	Monday	Tuesday	Wednesday	Thursday	Friday	Saturday
12–1 AM							
1–2 AM							
2–3 AM							
3–4 AM							
4–5 AM							
5–6 AM							
6–7 AM							
7–8 AM							
8–9 AM							
9–10 AM							
10–11 AM							
11–12 AM							
12–1 PM							
1–2 PM							
2–3 PM							
3–4 PM							
4–5 PM							
5–6 PM							
6–7 PM							
7–8 PM							
8–9 PM							
9–10 PM							
10–11 PM							
11–12 PM							

Figure 3.1 ■ Perceived Schedule

Time	Sunday	Monday	Tuesday	Wednesday	Thursday	Friday	Saturday
12–1 AM							
1–2 AM							
2–3 AM							
3–4 AM							
4–5 AM							
5–6 AM							
6–7 AM							
7–8 AM							
8–9 AM							
9–10 AM							
10–11 AM							
11–12 AM							
12–1 PM							
1–2 PM							
2–3 PM							
3–4 PM							
4–5 PM							
5–6 PM							
6–7 PM							
7–8 PM							
8–9 PM							
9–10 PM							
10–11 PM							
11–12 PM							

Figure 3.2 ▪ Actual Schedule

Step 2: Write down the specific activities that you want to do that match your choices.

Step 3: Note how much time each week you want to spend on each activity.

Activity 3: Evaluate a Weekly Schedule

It is helpful to set up a daily schedule of your time availability so you can use your time effectively. This schedule is a guideline, not an unbreakable "rule."

Objectives: (1) To prioritize your major responsibilities; (2) to use the time available to you effectively; (3) to evaluate the schedule you have made.

Procedure: Group activity

Step 1: Study the daily schedule below for Julie, a single parent with a four-year-old son named Johnny. Julie wants to get an associate degree as a veterinary assistant. She has always liked animals and has enjoyed "pet sitting" for friends and neighbors. She is returning to school after five years as a receptionist in an animal hospital. Her parents support her decision and care for her son while she attends classes. They are also helping her financially. Julie wants to complete her degree as quickly as possible in order to lift some of the responsibility from her parents' shoulders. She is taking two college classes and working nine hours a week at the college. Here is her schedule:

Julie's Daily Schedule

6:30 A.M.	Wake up, get dressed, get Johnny ready to go to Mom and Dad's house
7:00 A.M.	Prepare and eat breakfast with Johnny
7:30 A.M.	Take Johnny to Mom and Dad's
8:00 A.M.	Go to work at the college
11:00 A.M.	Go home, take the dog out, eat lunch
1:00 P.M.	Class
2:30 P.M.	Run errands
3:30 P.M.	Class
4:45 P.M.	Pick up Johnny from Mom and Dad's house
5:30 P.M.	Prepare and eat supper with Johnny
6:00 P.M.	Take a walk and/or spend time with Johnny
8:00 P.M.	Read Johnny a bedtime story and put him to bed
8:30 P.M.	Study and do homework
11:00 P.M.	Go to bed

Step 2: In small groups, suggest ways that Julie could modify her schedule to allow for more balance. Is there anything that is missing from her schedule? Is there anything that she could cut from her daily schedule? What other suggestions would you offer?

Activity 4: Create a New Weekly Schedule

You now have a better sense of how to make effective time management decisions. This exercise will help you implement these new insights.

Objectives: (1) Learn to put your priorities and values into action; (2) create a realistic new schedule.

Procedure:

Step 1: Using the format shown in Figure 3.3 (see page 21) as a guideline, set up a new master schedule for yourself.

Step 2: Evaluate your new schedule using the following questions:

1. Have you included your highest priority items?
2. Have you scheduled your most challenging tasks during your best hours as far as possible?
3. Does your schedule reflect a balance of time for yourself, your family and friends, and your responsibilities?
4. Is your schedule flexible?
5. Does the schedule reflect your values?
6. Do you want to rethink anything in your schedule? Can you combine any activities? Consider alternatives? Cut back or expand on anything?
7. Do you need to involve significant people in your life to support you in carrying out this schedule?

Time	Sunday	Monday	Tuesday	Wednesday	Thursday	Friday	Saturday
12–1 AM							
1–2 AM							
2–3 AM							
3–4 AM							
4–5 AM							
5–6 AM							
6–7 AM							
7–8 AM							
8–9 AM							
9–10 AM							
10–11 AM							
11–12 AM							
12–1 PM							
1–2 PM							
2–3 PM							
3–4 PM							
4–5 PM							
5–6 PM							
6–7 PM							
7–8 PM							
8–9 PM							
9–10 PM							
10–11 PM							
11–12 PM							

Figure 3.3 ■ Master Schedule

8. What kind of planning/scheduling book or electronic time management device are you using or do you want to use? When will you obtain it?
9. Will planning your time help you to take control of your life by confronting unproductive patterns of behavior, such as laziness, procrastination, and denial? Do you need to adjust the schedule so that it does?
10. Does your schedule support you to be a balanced person and a successful student and employee?
11. Does your schedule allow enough time for unforeseen possibilities?

Step 3: Share your schedule with others in your class or in a small group. Using their feedback, are there any other changes you need to make?

JOURNAL FOR SUCCESS

Journal Entry

Objective: To become more aware of how taking command of your time through planning and understanding of what you value, what is really important to you, brings about genuine success in achieving what you want and need.

Procedure: Upon completing all or any of the previous activities, describe what the experience was like for you and what are the implications for your future success.

CHAPTER 4
Success in Managing Stress

One cannot manage too many affairs; like pumpkins in the water,
one pops up while you try to hold down the other.

—Chinese proverb

To Learn and Understand

- How can you tell when your stress level is unhealthy?
- How can you handle negative stressful situations in your life?
- Do you want to simplify your life? How?

4.1 OUR STRESSFUL ENVIRONMENT

Some social scientists say the progress we in the United States have made in technological advances seems to be a double-edged sword, bringing benefits but also both positive and negative stress. We relish the challenges and success in making our lives easier, yet anxieties and frustrations occupy our lives, and we seem to be working harder than ever. It's almost impossible to find quiet time away from phones and computers. The Internet is an information superhighway, but it is almost overwhelming in size, speed, and problematic complexities.

At home, parents are facing multiple roles as their children's expectations of a continuous round of activities grow. Caregivers in homes and institutions are exhausted and in need of care themselves. In the work world, employees and employers alike are putting in more hours while often experiencing less satisfaction. Students, while trying to focus on their studies, also balance college with work, family, and social activities.

Here is Nancy's description of immense stress that she is experiencing in her life.

> I'm really no different than anyone else in the world. Lots of responsibilities, lots of demands on my time, lots of stress as a result. But for me, it isn't that there is a lot. The stress comes from knowing that it will never end. No matter how many hours I work, how long I stay up, how early I get up, how many tasks I complete, there is always more, more, more. I never get to the end. I have never been able to say, "There, everything I needed to take care of is all done, so I'll just sit down and relax." IT IS NEVER ALL DONE! Day after day there is no end in sight. In fact, it seems the pile grows faster than I can do the work, the chores, make all the calls, write all the papers necessary, complete all the business contacts. . . . For me, that is the most difficult part—getting discouraged because I can't ever finish. The stress of that can really get me down. So, instead of dreaming that I'll actually ever get it all done, I try to focus on being happy with what I have managed today. But I absolutely know, when I am on my deathbed, some voice will say, "No, you can't go now, you're not finished with all of this yet!"

4.2 IDENTIFYING STRESS

There are two kinds of stress: positive and negative. **Positive stress** can be associated with positive events, such as the stress of anticipation before a 10K run, an exciting trip, or giving a music recital. Such anticipation energizes you to rise to the occasion and put forth your best effort toward achievement or fun. It enables you to function effectively and to be successful.

In contrast, **negative stress,** which is characterized by physical, mental, and emotional consequences such as sleepless nights, preoccupation, or anger can be highly destructive. This kind of stress can cause your body to respond in an unhealthy way, with muscle tension, migraine headaches, or other illnesses. Concentration and performance both suffer. Hence, by definition, negative stress is dysfunctional and harmful.

Psychologists identify major life changes as negative stress-producing. They cite examples such as the death of a spouse/significant person; divorce; loss of a job; starting at a new school; living in a violent environment; moving; physical pain; or too much work, as Nancy described above. In addition to these major stressors, we encounter small negative stress episodes almost daily.

As an example, in the supermarket, a person with thirty items is in the ten-item-maximum express line ahead of you. The checkout person begins to run the customer's order through. How do you respond? Are you boiling with anger inside? Do you say something about the situation? Do you shrug it off as just "one of those things?" Depending on your type of personality and how much stress has already happened in your day, your response might vary.

It is important that you look at your response to stress. If it seems to be out of proportion to the event, there may also be another stress underlying your reaction. That underlying stress also needs to be given attention. What is really causing your stress?

4.3 SUCCESSFUL SIMPLIFYING STRATEGIES

Each of us knows our own situation, responsibilities, challenges, and dreams. Each of us will have a different experience. Perhaps you can use some of the following ideas to help you in your search for a less stressful, more harmonious life.

1. Block out times on your calendar for fun and relaxation.
2. De-clutter your environment.
3. Have voice mail or an answering machine take your calls so you can answer them all at once, instead of handling constant interruptions.
4. Hug a friend.
5. Negotiate more reasonable deadlines for school or work assignments.
6. Close your eyes and breathe deeply and slowly five times through your nose and expanding your belly instead of your chest, breathing in relaxation and breathing out stress.
7. Imagine being in your favorite place, perhaps in the woods, alone by a lake, or on the crest of a mountain, spending time perceiving the beauty of nature.
8. Close your eyes for five minutes.

9. Watch fish swim in an aquarium or observe any nature scene where there are birds, squirrels, chip-munks, or other animals.
10. Pet an animal.
11. Play relaxing music.
12. Take a brisk walk.
13. Stretch.
14. Read a few pages of a book you are interested in.
15. Have a healthy snack.
16. Pick up the phone and talk to someone special in your life.
17. Yawn.
18. Meditate.
19. Get a massage.
20. Buy some flowers.

Esther Orioli, chief executive officer of Essi Systems, a stress research and health consulting firm in San Francisco, writes in *The Stress Map*: "When you're dying from a heart attack, you can blame your employer, but you're the one in the hospital. You're going to say, 'Why didn't I take better care of myself?' It's time to stick your toe into the risk zone and stand up for yourself."

■ TIPS FOR SUCCESS ■
Managing Stress

1. Let go of unrealistic expectations for yourself.
2. Attend to your health needs.
3. Deal with one experience at a time without trying to control the shape of the outcome.
4. Make time to play and don't take yourself so seriously.
5. Slow down.
6. Remind yourself that your worth lies in who you are and not in what you do.
7. Make financial decisions that give you peace of mind.
8. Make friends with people who share similar values with you so you don't need to be in conflict with others.
9. List the things for which you are grateful in your life.
10. Evaluate and understand your needs. Be aware when you have unmet needs, and take steps to address them.
11. Be willing to ask for assistance. Enable others to help you (see Chapter 1).
12. Be available to support others.
13. Plan your time according to your values (see Chapter 3).
14. Be aware of becoming unbalanced by stress and take steps to regain your balance.
15. Remember the three R's: *respect* yourself, *respect* others, and take *responsibility* for all your actions.

SCENARIO FOR SUCCESS

Takanimi Nako has learned to work hard for his success. He got through college not taking time for fun. Now at work his coworkers perceive him as serious, intense, and often uptight and angry with them. Some days every muscle in his body hurts from trying to work so hard. His manager counsels him to ease up and lighten up, or he could lose his job.

Takanimi decides he has to make some changes. His first action is to walk half an hour every lunch hour. After the first week, he begins to invite his coworkers to join him. When there are breaks at work to celebrate an employee's birthday, he leaves his desk and joins in the celebration instead of continuing to work. He now limits his workweek to no more than fifty hours.

Takanimi's blood pressure drops back to normal, and the pains in his body go away. He is starting to have relationships with his coworkers instead of isolating them by seeing them all as lazy and less committed than he is. His job regains its security.

Questions for Discussion

1. Have you ever personally experienced stress overload similar to Takanimi Nako's? If so, what was the situation and what did you do about it? How were your strategies different from his?
2. Which of the simplifying strategies or tips for success from this chapter have you been using effectively to manage the negative stressors in your life? What have been the results?
3. What are the positive stressors you are experiencing that are enhancing your life?

ACTIVITIES FOR SUCCESS

Activity 1: Stress Management

Alternative relaxation techniques, some from ancient Eastern traditions, are becoming known in the United States and are gaining in popularity as methods of stress reduction.

Objectives: (1) To learn about alternative relaxation techniques; (2) to experiment with a technique that appeals to you.

Procedure:

Step 1: Select one of the following relaxation techniques and research how it works. Check on its availability in your area.

Note: *Do not participate in these without medical approval. Some medical conditions could be worsened.*

acupressure	herbal treatment	progressive relaxation
aromatherapy	hypnotism	reflexology
biofeedback	kinesiology	reiki
chakra balancing	massage	Tai Chi Chuan
guided imagery	meditation	Yoga

Step 2: Make a report to your class, providing the following information:
  1. What is the history of the technique?
  2. How does the technique contribute to relaxation?
  3. What evidence of success can you cite?
  4. Have you used the technique yourself, or do you know someone who has? With what results?
  5. Where can students access the technique?

JOURNAL FOR SUCCESS

Journal Entry

As your life changes, the amount of support you want and need from others changes too. From time to time it is a good idea to assess your own support environment. The exercises below will help you to identify areas of support, what further support you may need, and how to go about gaining that support.

Objectives: (1) To assess your support environment; (2) to evaluate what areas of support you want and need.

Procedure: Provide answers for each of the following:

1. List the first names of people who encourage, love, and support you, and then indicate how each person provides that support. Is it by listening to you? Offering suggestions? Helping financially? Sharing responsibilities with you? Sharing interests? Showing you that they care about you? Other ways?
2. Give examples of how you contribute to your own physical health.

3. Give examples of how you assert your rights.
4. Give examples of how you nurture your spiritual life.
5. Give examples of how you help your mind to continue to grow.
6. Give examples of how you affirm yourself for being a person of value and deserving respect.
7. In what area(s) do you see that you need more support?
8. What are some ways that you can help yourself to gain that support?

CHAPTER 5

Critical Thinking and Decision Making for Success

More powerful than the tread of mighty armies is the idea whose moment has come.

—Victor Hugo

To Learn and Understand

- What are the six steps to critical thinking?
- How do critical thinking skills expedite learning?
- Are you primarily an auditory learner, a visual learner, or a tactile learner?
- What actions lead to effective decisions?

5.1 SUCCESSFUL CRITICAL-THINKING SKILLS

Higher-level thinking often presents a challenge to students who may not have had enough practice in high school. Jamie, for example, wants to learn about how to use these thinking skills to succeed in test-taking. "I studied for five hours last night, and nothing I studied was on the test," Jamie complained to Ray. "I memorized the definitions of all the terms, but there were no definitions on the exam. Instead, the teacher gave us some case studies and asked us to select the best treatment in each case."

Jamie's complaint is a common one. Students often focus their areas of study at the level of memorization and comprehension. These two areas are essential to learning, but usually they aren't useful by themselves. While they form the basis for higher-level **critical thinking**, they tend to lead to **introjections**—swallowing whole what one reads or hears without exploring the information critically. Instead, students need to chew on ideas, like some animals chew their food, examining and questioning the data from every angle and considering the validity of the sources used. It is particularly helpful to make every effort to understand the motivations of those providing the information. For example, if certain information suggests the reason for a tax cut, you might consider whether the data were provided by a Republican or a Democrat, which might indicate a bias.

In *Taxonomy of Educational Objectives*, Benjamin Bloom suggests six steps to successful critical thinking:

1. Knowledge	4. Analysis
2. Comprehension	5. Synthesis
3. Application	6. Evaluation

Step 1: Knowledge

Knowledge of a subject is at the base of all the other thinking skills. Gathering accurate information is the foundation upon which the other thinking skills rest. Specific knowledge varies with a particular subject, but various types of knowledge include terminology, facts, sequences, categories, methods, and generalizations. For example, in Shakespeare's *Romeo and Juliet* we know these five facts:

Fact 1: Juliet says to Romeo, "Wherefore art thou Romeo?"
Fact 2: Romeo and Juliet come from two families who are feuding with each other.
Fact 3: The deaths of Romeo and Juliet bring the two families together.
Fact 4: The play is called a tragedy because of the unhappy ending.
Fact 5: Shakespeare uses many references to "fate" in the play, calling Romeo and Juliet "star-crossed lovers."

Step 2: Comprehension

Understanding what the information means is essential in learning and applying the knowledge. By translating or interpreting information, you illustrate that you comprehend what you have studied. For example, when you know that "wherefore" means "why" in that famous quotation from *Romeo and Juliet*, you are able to interpret the line correctly: "Romeo, Romeo, why is your name Romeo?"

Step 3: Application

An application may be a generalization about a given fact. For example, if you know that Romeo's family is feuding with Juliet's family, you may assume things will not be easy for the two lovers. The generalization could apply in other situations as well; for instance, if parents are going through a divorce, things are probably difficult for the children.

Step 4: Analysis

The thinking skill of analysis challenges you to bring together various understandings in order to predict a conclusion. The analysis enables you to understand different parts of an issue and the relationship between the parts. The better the analysis, the better the prediction. For example, Shakespeare calls Romeo and Juliet "star-crossed lovers." Such references to fate in the play provide clues about what may happen later.

Step 5: Synthesis

Synthesis means putting together elements and parts from a whole, such as the ability to write in an organized and creative way, or to put together a set of facts in such a way that a new outcome results. For example, Romeo and Juliet belong to families that are feuding with each other. Their deaths bring the two families together. One of Shakespeare's themes in the play involves a synthesis—the idea that tragedy can bring people together.

Step 6: Evaluation

The highest form of critical thinking is evaluation—forming judgments internally on the basis of evidence. Evaluation provides students with the opportunity to look at the information from individually unique perspectives. For example, even though you were provided with many references that foreshadowed the deaths of Romeo and Juliet, you continued to read the story, because you wanted to see and understand the details of what happened and evaluate the characters' choices.

These are the various levels of critical thinking skills. Like Jamie, the student who studied only at the level of memorization and comprehension, you can now increase your test-taking power by including critical thinking as part of your studying.

5.2 LEARNING STYLES

Research shows that students learn most easily when they can access their own learning style. There are many ways to categorize learning styles. One system describes learning styles in three ways: (1) auditory, (2) visual, or (3) tactile.

Auditory learners like to talk to someone about what they are learning. Explaining a concept or issue to someone else helps clarify their own thinking, just as listening to others express their ideas helps them understand and remember what they are trying to learn. Studying in a group is especially helpful to auditory learners.

Visual learners grasp concepts more easily by seeing them illustrated in graphs, charts, and photographs and using other visuals. They enhance their learning by organizing in lists, making eye contact with the lecturer, watching a film, and writing down what they are attempting to learn.

Tactile learners are those who learn best by doing. They are often in motion, restless when they are forced to sit and listen for long periods, eager to use their energy. Building models, drawing graphs, making charts—activities that allow them to use their kinetic energy enhance their learning process.

Most people use all three learning styles but, consciously or not, most have a predominant learning style. Think about how you learn best. Do you like to study alone or with a group? With background music or in a quiet setting? Do you like to move about when you study, or sit at your desk until you finish an assignment? Do you like to get feedback while you are working on a writing project, or are you reluctant to show it to anyone until you are finished? Do illustrations in textbooks help you to understand the content, or do they confuse you?

If you can discover whether you are an auditory, a visual, or a tactile learner, you can enhance your learning process by choosing activities that support your learning style. You can also choose instructors, when possible, who tend to teach the way you learn best. Here are some suggestions for each of the three types of learners:

1. Auditory Learners
   - Tape the professor's lectures (with permission) to listen to them again later.
   - Compose a song or parody to help you retain key concepts.
   - Recite information out loud.
   - Read aloud whenever possible.
   - Study with others, taking turns asking questions.

2. Visual Learners
   - Compare class notes with classmates.
   - Use a highlighter to emphasize ideas, key terms, and phrases.
   - Use reference graphs, illustrations, and charts as sources of information.
   - Use symbols such as underlining, circles, boxes, exclamation marks, or checks to call attention to important words.
   - Look at the speaker in a lecture situation. Take notes only to summarize.
   - Sit close to the speaker and away from distractions.
   - Make flash cards.
   - Illustrate key concepts with drawing or doodling.
   - Study alone.
   - Practice visualizing or picturing important information, making a "movie" in your mind.
   - Color-code notes to help you to visualize by association.
   - Use the "loci" method of the ancient Romans, in which you imagine a house or room, and place pictures of the items you want to remember in various locations.

3. Tactile Learners
   - In class, make movements that will not disturb the class but will help you remain alert, such as rolling a pencil, squeezing an eraser, or flexing a muscle.
   - Take frequent notes; write important facts repeatedly while studying.
   - After class, create movements or dance steps that seem to express the theme of the class or a concept you want to remember.
   - Construct a chart, a poster, or a model of the material you are studying.

5.3 EFFECTIVE DECISION MAKING

Every moment of every waking day you make choices about your actions. The quality of these choices is directly dependent upon the effectiveness of your skills in analyzing information and coming to a decision that is the best for yourself and others. Many decisions are minor, with few if any negative consequences tied to either choice. It is unlikely to make any difference to anyone, for instance, if you choose cream cheese for your morning bagel instead of strawberry jam!

When it comes to decisions that have greater impact, however, it is important to do the following:

1. Pause.
2. Gather facts.
3. Analyze the facts to determine their accuracy.
4. Get input from others who are affected by the decision or who care about you (see Chapter 12).

No decision is perfect. If you find you made a wrong choice—change direction! Your career, health, or family are far too important to take this process lightly.

A word of caution: Sometimes it is very easy to believe everything you read, hear, and see. At times you will need to look at other sources of information to compare and analyze the facts. This is especially true if your source of information is the Internet, where anyone can post anything. When relying on other people for information, it is also important to assess your level of trust in them. This does not mean approaching others distrustfully. It is important to approach people expecting the best from them. However, it is just as important to pay attention to clues and facts that indicate caution. How has your new boyfriend treated others? Have you checked the references of someone you are about to hire? Are you sure you are getting good advice from school counselors to assist you with appropriate course choices?

Being discriminating, questioning, discovering, and exploring before making a decision will result in effective decisions. By using careful and analytical thinking skills, thoughtful people accept and process facts, accepting what is true and plausible, and discarding false or misleading information.

Let's say you are examining your options in the workplace. You are happy with your job—good pay, adequate benefits, interesting work. Few jobs, however, are secure forever. Companies sell out or merge with other companies, or they restructure and downsize in a way that eliminates jobs. If you hear a rumor about layoffs, it is wise for you to gather facts quickly and decide on a course of action. Perhaps you will stay and see what happens. Analysis might lead you to a decision, however, to accept a position with another company.

■ TIPS FOR SUCCESS ■
Critical Thinking and Decision Making

1. Apply your knowledge and experience to evaluate what you read and hear.
2. Use resources such as books, the Internet, experts, and programs on educational television to expand your knowledge about areas you are involved in studying.
3. Set up a filing system by subjects of interest to you and make a point to read and file information for use in the future.
4. Use written lists of positive and negative aspects of areas under discussion or decisions to be made.
5. Involve others in discussions about topics and decisions to hear different points of view.
6. Follow the four steps that lead to effective decision making (see Section 5.3).

SCENARIO FOR SUCCESS

Rini Zahowski is a software developer in the fast-paced world of e-commerce. This area changes on a daily basis, so she has been required to keep informed of changes by regular reading. Each week her goal is to read at least three magazines in this field. She marks articles that are the most interesting in each. At least one day a week she arranges to have lunch with a colleague, and together they go through the articles and discuss the content and how it applies to their work. She clips articles of special interest and saves them filed by subject so she can refer to them in the future.

Questions for Discussion

1. What do you think of Rini's efforts to keep pace with enormous changes in her industry? Does her experience remind you of anything in your life?
2. How can you better use the tips for success above to critically think through the challenges in your life? Have you any other ideas to add?
3. Have you noticed any incidents in your life recently that demonstrate you have been less gullible and more discriminating in the things you hear, read, and see on television? How do you account for this change in behavior?

ACTIVITIES FOR SUCCESS

Activity 1: Critical Thinking and Making Decisions

Using critical thinking during studying improves your effectiveness in doing assignments and taking tests.

Objective: To practice critical thinking.

Procedure: Work in small groups.

Step 1: Read the following selection critically, evaluating the arguments for logic and identifying unstated assumptions.

Peggy, a junior in college, and David, a small business owner, have spirited arguments about a state law that requires motorcyclists to wear helmets when operating their vehicles. "Helmets are a nuisance, especially in hot weather," says Peggy. A free-spirited person, she gets a rush of excitement as she goes down the interstate highway at sixty miles an hour with the wind blowing through her hair. The helmet law interferes with her personal liberty, she says.

"Yes," replies David. "As do a lot of other laws—like traveling 20 mph in a school zone, or making sure that when small children ride in your car they sit in the back seat and are strapped in. But they protect people from being hurt."

Peggy listened, but she was not convinced until David read her a newspaper article about a college student who wasn't wearing a helmet and crashed his motorcycle into a tree. He was in a coma for six years before he finally died.

"Peggy, you're a math major," David said. "How much do you think it cost to keep that guy on life support for six years?"

"Probably a thousand dollars a day—at least $365,000 a year," Peggy answered. "Wow, that's more than 2 million for six years!"

"And guess what," said David. "The guy had no insurance. Who do you think paid the bill?"

"The taxpayers, I guess."

"You're right. Just remember that some of us taxpayers don't like to pay for hospital stays just so you can feel the wind in your hair."

Step 2: Discuss the following questions:

1. What is David's opinion about the helmet law?
2. Are his arguments logical?
3. What are his unstated assumptions?
4. What do you think of Peggy's position in the beginning?
5. What do you think she decided about wearing a helmet?
6. What decision would you make?

Activity 2: Prioritizing Learning Styles

Objective: To apply your understanding of your learning style preference.

Procedure:

Step 1: The teaching process usually includes visual and auditory approaches, and sometimes the tactile learning style as well. The order in which these learning styles are presented may depend on your teacher's learning preference. Suppose you—as a teacher—had to teach the structure of the human

brain. Decide in what order you would introduce information based on your own learning style preference. For example, would you first give the students a model of the human brain and ask them to take it
apart and replace the lobes correctly (tactile)? Or would you begin by telling the students about the
structure of the brain (auditory)? Or would you show them a chart of the brain's structure (visual)?
Explain the reasons for your choices.

Step 2: Consider the choices you made in Step 1. Now select a challenging class you are currently taking.
Analyze the usual teaching style of the professor in that class. Does the teacher's process fit your learning
style preference? If it doesn't, consider how you can modify your own approach to learning (see Section
5.2 for ideas). For example, if you need a more auditory approach, consider asking the professor if you
may tape record the class. If you prefer a hands-on approach, you might want to make flashcards, or
you may want to supplement the class presentation with models or other apparatus available for student
use. If you prefer the visual approach, you may want to recopy or redraft the notes you have taken as a
review technique. Share your results with classmates.

JOURNAL FOR SUCCESS

Journal Entry 1

Objective: To determine the applicability of your learning style in terms of critical thinking.

Procedure: Consider all the information you have gathered about your preferred learning style. Write in
your journal an analysis of that information. What confirms what you already know about your preferred
learning style? What new insights have you gained? How will you implement what you have learned into
your life?

Journal Entry 2

Objective: To apply critical-thinking steps to a personal decision.

Procedure: Choose one of the tasks below, whichever is most applicable to your life. Write out all your options and the decision you end up making. Draft a plan of action to fulfill the decision in clear, concise steps.

1. With vacation soon approaching, what are your options for finding a job over break? Is money the only issue? Would a field experience or internship enhance your resume and give you job skills for the future?
   What critical questions do you need to ask yourself to help you develop an action plan?

2. If you are currently working, what are your options for advancement, or do you want to change to a
   new job?

CHAPTER 6
Thinking Creatively for Success

Like the pure spring that bubbles out of the rock unbidden ... creativity has no necessity and no end, and pervades all of existence.

—F. David Peat

To Learn and Understand

- What is creativity?
- What can you do to promote creativity in your life?

6.1 CREATIVE THINKING

You might wonder, "How am I a creator?" **Creative energy** takes many forms, from solving a household problem to writing a short story to masterminding the engineering of a bridge. Often we do not recognize the creativity within us, or we may view the word "creative" in the narrower context of performers and artists. Looking at creativity from a broader perspective, we can begin to appreciate the many applications of creativity in our lives.

Marilyn, a participant in an employment retraining program, explains creativity in this way: "Creativity comes from experience. It comes from the inside and what you have gone through in life. I need peace and quiet in order to be creative, but I also need examples to start me on my way."

Some people need a creative environment to get the juices flowing. Jennie, a student at a technical school, finds it rejuvenating to be out in nature: "A friend of mine has a nice piece of property out in the country. When I go there, it is so quiet I can actually hear the birds and smell the flowers. My head clears, and I can relax and feel the stress and pressure leave my body so the ideas can enter in. In the past fifteen years that I have been on my own as an adult, I can't remember one situation I have been in that I have not been able to creatively work my way through."

Jia, a freelance newsletter writer, finds that "the best place for me to write is in my bedroom lying on my comfortable bed. It seems to be more quiet there than anywhere else. I sometimes tend to make big things out of little things. I really need to slow down. My mind races, and I can get easily frustrated. Pausing to rest quietly helps me with all these things."

Returning to school after several years, Emanuel describes his new perspective: "The dreams and the goals I set for myself give me a wide range of possibilities. Because of freethinking, creative ideas are suddenly emerging in my head. When my back is against the wall, I tend to excel. I live for pressure situations."

Roger von Oech, author of *A Whack on the Side of the Head*, admits that most of what we do doesn't require much creativity. The problem is, he explains, that when we need to be creative, often "our own attitudes can get in the way." He suggests that to open these locks and free your creativity, you first need to recognize them in yourself, then "temporarily forget them when you are trying to generate ideas." Von Oech lists ten mental locks that can stifle creativity:

1. Looking for the right answer
2. Always trying to be logical
3. Strictly following the rules
4. Insisting on being practical
5. Avoiding ambiguity
6. Fearing and avoiding failure
7. Forgetting how to play
8. Becoming too specialized
9. Not wanting to look foolish
10. Saying, "I'm not creative"

Guidelines for Successful Creativity

Creative thinking skills are powerful tools in our everyday lives, our work lives, and our school lives. When we dare to break out of our usual thinking patterns and let our creative juices flow, we are far more likely to generate new ideas, discover innovative solutions to problems, and bring energy and excitement to our activities. Here are some guidelines to follow:

1. *Seeing differently and being aware:* We are such creatures of habit that often we do not recognize change when we see it. Expecting to see the usual, we do not see the unusual. By focusing on seeing differently, we open up new and interesting perspectives. Travel, conversation, reading, reflection, education, and writing—all are ways to see things from a different point of view. Seeing differently sets the stage for the mind to configure an environment or a problem in a new and creative way.

2. *The whole is greater than its parts:* An object when broken down into component parts, may be reassembled in such a way that it serves a different function. For example, a metal clothes hanger in its original form is designed to hold a piece of clothing. However, when it is twisted out of shape to resemble a hook, it may be used to retrieve an object in an enclosed place or to scratch a person's back.

3. *Never assume:* In *Desk Set,* a classic film written by Garson Kanin and Ruth Gordon, actor Spencer Tracy tests the intelligence of his co-star, Katharine Hepburn. He tells her the following story and asks her to determine who killed Harry and Grace. Here are the clues: A detective entered the plush Fifth Avenue apartment. In the living room, on the floor, was a puddle of water. Beside the water were two goldfish, dead. On the table stood a cat, his back arched. Who killed Harry and Grace?

   As long as we assume that Harry and Grace are people, we are unable to solve the mystery. But if we let go of that assumption, we realize that Harry and Grace are the dead goldfish and that the cat committed the crime.

4. *The answer is within:* Dorothy knew she had met Ramon, the student sitting next to her in psychology class, but she could not recall where. After class she smiled at him. He returned the smile and asked if she had decided on a topic for her research essay. Dorothy said she wasn't sure what she wanted to do yet, but she was leaning toward investigating memory loss. After class, she thought to herself, I could combine my research with my own experience in not remembering where I met Ramon before. That night, before going to sleep, Dorothy closed her eyes, visualized Ramon's face, and heard his voice again. Then she fell asleep. The next morning, as soon as she awoke, she remembered where she had met Ramon. He was a friend of her brother's, and she had given him a ride to high school a couple of times. That settled it for Dorothy. She chose the topic of how the memory works.

5. *Recycled ideas create new ones:* Carole, a freelance journalist, did extensive research on a company for an article. When the article was published, she combined her research with research on another company, which gave her a whole new angle for another story. At the same time, she heard about a project to develop a Website of references for businesses in her city. Again, Carole was able to use many of her findings and funnel them into a new medium. She sold her material to the fledgling Web company, which allowed her to use her research a third time.

6. *Expect the unexpected:* Expecting the unexpected is helpful when a student is working on a creative project such as computer programming. Chris, a programming student, attributes his success to letting go of expectations. He explains: "I have totally different strategies to come up with creative ideas for projects and solving problems. I start by thinking of the most wild and unique ideas I can. Then, I try to program the structure to fit the ideas. It all turns out much differently than if I start with the structure first."

6.2 CREATIVE CONNECTIONS AND PATTERNS

Renee finds that her creative ideas come from associating ordinary events and circumstances in newly connected patterns. She explains the process this way:

> When asked to create metaphors in my journal entry, I connected the words supplied to current events in my own life. When asked to freely associate with the word "asphalt," a chain effect was created. My first association was with street workers. This led me to my past history classes,

where I learned the government would employ street workers to help the economy. I then recalled that they did this to jump-start the economy. Thus, my final response: the economy.

In free associating with the word "tennis," I derived "financial aid." This was also accomplished through word association. You see, tennis made me think of Elizabeth, who was a star tennis player in my high school. She is the daughter of my college advisor. This reminded me that I needed to complete my financial aid forms.

I have also found that I discover some of my best creative solutions when I am in unfamiliar surroundings. This fosters the use of my creative thinking ability by enabling me to connect the new surroundings and events to those familiar to me.

6.3 WAYS TO ACCESS YOUR CREATIVITY

There are many ways to get creativity flowing. Some of these are outlined below, but use your creativity, and you may discover many more.

1. *Physical activity:* Jogging, brisk walking, taking a shower, driving, or working out—these are some physical activities that people use to release their creativity. Brad, an entrepreneur, says he finds creativity by working out to burn off stress or by floating around lakes in his sailboat. "Now that's an idea—a floating gym on the lake. I could solve the world's problems," he said.

2. *Pressure:* Denise, a shipping coordinator for a busy manufacturing company, finds that having a deadline for pickup prompts her creativity. "I have to figure out new ways to get products ready and new packaging techniques all the time."

3. *Quiet time:* Quiet times usually help people in their creative processing. Businesses recognize that providing employees with time to relax gets their creative juices going. In "How to Nurture Creative Sparks," an article in *Fortune* about creativity in business, writers Alan Farnham and Joyce E. Davis describe a creative approach to quiet time: "At Hallmark, whose more than 600 artists, writers, and designers constitute what they claim is the largest creative staff in the world. . .writers and artists. . .get sent on what seem like vacations to soak up atmosphere and inspiration."

4. *Taking notes:* Peggy, a customer service supervisor at a chemical company, likes to take notes and then integrate them into creative ideas. She explains, "To come up with ideas, I create lists of notations. I may have these lists in my desk, my car, my purse, just about anywhere. I then take my ideas and group them together. Then I see how many things can be created from each topic. After I see which one I can be the most creative with (there may be two or three), I write something under each one. The creativity flows."

5. *Napping:* Chen, a college instructor, prepares for each class a day or two in advance, and then "sleeps" on the ideas. Like clockwork, after a refreshing twenty-minute nap, the ideas gel, and Chen's lesson is creatively integrated, perhaps by his subconscious mind. It is easy for him to complete his lesson planning. A nap provides needed rest for the body, mind, and spirit. Napping is an opportunity to do something for ourselves, a simple way to recharge our batteries and boost our energy.

6. *Using the nondominant hand:* In *The Power of Your Other Hand*, Lucia Capacchione traces some research and results of writing with a person's nondominant hand: "When you realize that the nondominant hand, usually the left hand, is governed by the right hemisphere in most people, it is no surprise that the qualities ascribed to the right brain—creative, emotional, intuitive—are precisely the qualities that come out most easily when the nondominant hand writes."

   Capacchione suggests that we write with the nondominant hand to surface emotions, to talk through ideas, to bring out artistic and creative ideas, and to resolve personal issues.

   Because we are so new at writing with the nondominant hand, we need to be patient and attentive when first writing in this unaccustomed way. Initially, people feel vulnerable and at-risk, because their writing may look scribbled and unintelligible. However, with practice, the nondominant hand's writing will improve, and the writer will feel more confident to experiment.

7. *Drawing with your dominant hand:* Drawing with your dominant hand can also aid in your creativity. Besides being an outlet for fun or a break from routine, it also enables you to engage in "mapping out" pictures, ideas, or images that are in your mind. With little or no structure needed, it allows freedom of movement and expression with strong neuromuscular connection between the brain and the hand.

■ **TIPS FOR SUCCESS** ■
Creative Thinking

1. Think "outside the box." Always look for innovative solutions.
2. Take different routes home from work and school and sit in a different seat in class each day. Find other ways to break up the routines in your life.
3. In activities, pair up with people you perceive as very creative and learn all you can from them.
4. Nurture your creativity by incorporating creative activities into your life, such as drawing, writing, and listening to and playing music.
5. Allow time for meditation and quiet to talk to yourself. Ask yourself questions and listen for creative answers.
6. Pay attention to your dreams. They often provide valuable insights.
7. Each day spend fifteen minutes doing nothing, preferably in a natural setting with no other people around.

SCENARIO FOR SUCCESS

Kerri O'Donnell works as an assistant editor for *Scrumptious*, a weekly newsletter for the restaurant industry. She is responsible for generating new and creative ideas each week about interesting foods, service improvements, and innovative marketing ideas. She has a marker board in her office with pens of different colors. She uses these to draw and jot down possibilities as they occur to her. Around the walls of her office she has posters of different foods and famous restaurants, and she keeps a notebook and pen by her bed for late-night brainstorms. Each week, she eats at a new restaurant to collect ideas. She also pins on her wall reviews of various restaurants that describe creative ideas. All of these things stimulate her to develop unique newsletters.

Questions for Discussion

1. Do you find that any of Kerri's techniques for being creative in her job might serve as a catalyst for nurturing your own creativity?
2. What techniques have you used to be more creative? What were the outcomes?
3. What was one of your most creative moments, and what helped to make it happen?

ACTIVITIES FOR SUCCESS

Activity 1: Creative Thinking

Creative thinking can help you develop a variety of endings to a situation or story.

Objective: To create multiple possible endings to a story.
Procedure: Group activity
   Step 1: Watch the first thirty minutes of a movie video you have not seen before with a small group of classmates.
   Step 2: Stop the video.
   Step 3: Discuss and write down five possible endings to the story.
   Step 4: Watch the rest of the video. Discuss with each other whether the ending was different from or similar to the ones you created in Step 3 and in what ways.

Activity 2: Accessing Your Creative Side

Looking at a situation from a different perspective can help you to access your creative side.

Objectives: (1) To view a situation from a different perspective; (2) to access your creativity.
Procedure: Group activity
    Step 1: As a group, go to a building that has multiple doors, windows, and levels.
    Step 2: The front door is an obvious way to escape from this building if it is on fire. Make a list of all other possible ways to escape from the building (minimum of ten).
    Step 3: Go to a room of the building and decide on your escape route if the fire starts in another part of the building.

Activity 3: Developing Your Creativity

Objectives: (1) To experiment with an art form that is new and different to you; (2) to heighten awareness of your creative side by developing an artistic skill.
Procedure:
    Step 1: Devote at least one uninterrupted hour to doing an art form that appeals to you. Figure 6.1 will provide you with some ideas. If you are already familiar with one art form, choose a different one for this experiment.
    Step 2: After spending time experimenting with the art form you chose, answer each of the following questions. Keep this, since your instructor may ask you to share the results of your artistic experiment with the class.
        1. Describe the art.
        2. How did you begin?
        3. How did the experiment develop?
        4. What did you learn about the art from your experience?
        5. What did you learn about yourself from the experience?

Writing	Poem	Joke	Greeting card	Drama	Short story	Article
Drawing	Cartoon	Sketch of a person	Sketch of a building	Abstract	Still life	Logo
Dancing	Choreography	Swing	Line	Ballroom	Jazz	Freestyle
Music	Write a song	Form a band	Attend a concert	Play an instrument	Listen to an orchestra	Make a recording
Cooking	Create a new recipe	Cater an event	Entertain	Cook a new dish	Decorate a cake	Try a new spice
Painting	Watercolor	Acrylic	Charcoal	Oil	Pastel	Silkscreen
Crafts	Woodwork	Quilting	Memory album	Embroidery	Stencil	Knit or crochet
Video	Direct	Produce	Film	Write script	Develop story line	Edit film
Gardening	Design a flower garden	Buy seeds or plants	Make an herb garden	Dry flowers	Arrange flowers	Pull weeds
Architecture	Design	Draft	Build	Choose colors	Furnish	Choose pictures for walls

Figure 6.1   ▪   Experimenting with Art Forms

JOURNAL FOR SUCCESS

Journal Entry 1

Some people believe they are not creative. Careful reflection might show otherwise.

Objective: Identify ways you are creative.

Procedure:

Step 1: Spend fifteen minutes in quiet reflection about ways you might be creative. Do not do this with other people around or while listening to music that has words.

Step 2: Write a journal entry answering the following questions:

1. Describe some ways you demonstrate creativity.
2. What mental, emotional, physical, spiritual, and environmental conditions and factors help you to be creative?
3. What areas of creativity do you appreciate in others?
4. What could you do to increase your creativity?

Journal Entry 2

Objectives: (1) To apply guidelines for successful creativity as alternative problem-solving strategies; (2) to integrate various perspectives in order to see the problem from a different level of awareness.

Procedure:

Step 1: Select one of the six guidelines for successful creativity (see Section 6.1).

Step 2: Explain how this guideline has led to a creative solution to a problem in your life.

Step 3: Look at a new problem in your life. What guideline(s) can you use to help you resolve it? How can you apply the guideline?

CHAPTER 7
Successful Note-Taking Methods

The human brain is not equipped to accept a constant flow of information.

—Martin Schuster

To Learn and Understand

- What is active listening?
- How can effectively taking notes help you in your classes?
- How can effectively taking notes help you in the workforce?
- What methods can you use to organize your lecture notes?
- What is active reading?

7.1 NOTE-TAKING SKILLS IN COLLEGE AND AT WORK

The key to successful study is being actively involved. When you are listening to a lecture or to a manager at a meeting, you need to keep the pen or laptop computer poised, ready to take down information and record questions that come to mind. Lecturers and other speakers use key words, tone of voice, visual aids, and repetition to reinforce key concepts. As an **active listener,** learn to identify those concepts and record them in your notes. If something is not clear to you, ask the speaker or your teacher to clarify the information. Do this as soon as possible to avoid going forward with false assumptions.

You are fortunate if you learned the value of effective note-taking skills early in your school life. New college students without those skills often become overwhelmed with the volume of information they are expected to absorb in reading assignments and in class lectures.

People embarking on new careers often experience the same feelings of information overload. Staying current in your career today usually requires reading articles by experts in your field, taking classes from time to time, attending conferences, and participating in company meetings. All of these activities require note-taking skills. If you are an active member of civic, religious, or social organizations, you can enhance your participation by taking effective notes or perhaps by taking the minutes of the meeting.

If you are using a note-taking system that works well for you and supports your learning style, you will probably want to continue using it. Perhaps you can enhance your methods, however, by learning two widely used and respected note-taking systems: the **Cornell note-taking system** and the **SQ3R study method.**

7.2 THE CORNELL NOTE-TAKING SYSTEM

The Cornell note-taking system was developed by Walter Pauk about forty years ago at Cornell University to help students better organize their notes. This system focuses primarily on taking notes for lecture classes, although it can be used for reading assignments as well. It is probably the most widely used system for taking notes in the United States. Many colleges teach it in their orientation classes for new students, and most college study-skill manuals include a section on it.

Preparation

To perform any process well, you need special tools. For the Cornell system, you need to use a notebook with paper that is large enough to divide into columns. Pauk suggests standard-size $8\frac{1}{2} \times 11$ inch loose-leaf paper kept in a three-ring binder. If you use a laptop computer to take notes, you can use the same format in appropriate proportions (see Figure 7.1).

The Cornell note-taking system uses the following structure:

- Section A (the largest area) is for taking notes during the lecture.
- Section B, called the cue column, is the section on the left side of the page, used for reducing notes to the most important ideas, facts, questions, and key words.
- Section C, the section across the bottom of the page, is for summarizing.

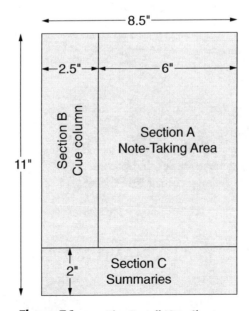

Figure 7.1 ■ The Cornell Note Sheet

During the lecture, record as many important ideas as you can in Section A. Be selective. If you try to write too much, you will miss important information. As you practice this method, you will sharpen your active listening skills (see Chapter 11). Active listening will in turn motivate you to ask appropriate questions and participate in class discussions, increasing your comprehension of the information and your enjoyment of the class.

Immediately after the lecture, or as soon as possible, record in Section B the most important ideas. This will reinforce memory, make concepts clearer to you, and raise questions about areas that are not clear to you.

Cover up Sections A and B and recite (aloud, if possible) in your own words the key concepts, facts, and words of the lecture. This is another opportunity to reinforce memory and clarify ideas.

As you go over your notes and cues, think about the ideas presented in the lecture. What is your opinion of some of those ideas? How do those ideas relate to your other courses or to your work or to what you have learned through reading or other experiences? If you keep a journal, you might consider entering these reflections there.

Write a brief summary of the lecture in Section C at the bottom of the page. Before a test, refer to the summary. If you have taken accurate notes, recorded key ideas, and reviewed material and reflected on it, just looking over your summary will help you recall important information and give you the confidence you need to do well on the test.

Do a quick review of your notes and recite important ideas at least once a week (but more often if possible). The more often you review, the more you will retain what you have learned.

This note-taking system will also serve you well in the workplace. Often people who attend meetings or training sessions are asked to present a summary of what they learned to coworkers at staff meetings. If you have a presentation to make to an important client, you will need to study materials, learn the key points, and communicate them clearly to the person. When you attend business meetings, you will need to make notes of key decisions and list items that require action when you return to your desk. Taking notes is definitely a lifetime skill.

7.3 SQ3R STUDY METHOD

Success in college and in many careers requires constant reading, which, without effective note-taking skills, can become a chore instead of the pleasure it can be. How do you cope with a textbook assignment? Are assignments harder to face each day? As you study a chapter from your textbook, do you become overwhelmed with the amount of information presented? You may benefit from a more systematic approach to textbook reading called **active reading**. One such approach is the SQ3R study method. This method was designed by Francis Robinson, a psychologist, to help military personnel undergoing accelerated university courses.

The name of the SQ3R method of study is derived from the following five words:

- Survey
- Question
- Read
- Recite
- Review

Some of the SQ3R steps are similar to those in the Cornell note-taking system. If you use the SQ3R method of study for your reading assignments, it might be a good idea to use the same three-ring binder and page formats (sections for taking notes, reducing them, and summarizing) that you use for your lecture notes. In this way, you can organize all material for a class in the same section.

SQ3R can help you to improve your reading concentration, speed, and memorization by becoming actively involved in the reading process. Textbook authors write from an outline and emphasize the important ideas. In fact, frequently, textbooks employ elements of the SQ3R method in the format of their books. When a textbook provides headings such as Preview, Objectives, Focus Questions, Summary, or Critical Thinking, the book is utilizing SQ3R study applications. The book you are reading right now, *College and Career Success Simplified*, uses SQ3R. This study method is based on research showing that students learn most effectively when they do the following:

- Take down information.
- Talk about information.
- See the big picture.

- Use questions to focus study time.
- Study a little at a time.
- Review information.
- Become actively involved in the learning process.

Survey

A surveyor is a person who scans the environment and sets up boundary measurements. In order to do the job effectively, the surveyor starts with a map of the total environment. This gives the surveyor the big or overall picture. Surveying a chapter in a textbook will enable you to get a sense of the big picture. Look at the chapter titles as well as any large print, boldface, and italicized headings. These are your "big picture" guideposts. Next, survey the illustrations, diagrams, and tables. You don't need to spend a long time on each graphic. Just take time to become familiar with the topic and picture the graphic in your mind. Lastly, look at the end of the chapter. Note any defined terms, questions for discussion, extension activities, and enrichment information. You will come back to this information later.

Question

There is power in questions. Asking focused questions guides your reading. If a textbook does not provide questions, you can make up your own by converting each heading into a question. The words below may help to get you thinking about questions and may help to prepare you for later tests and exams:

analyze	discuss	outline
comment on	enumerate	prove
compare	evaluate	relate
contrast	explain	review
criticize	illustrate	state
define	interpret	summarize
describe	justify	trace
diagram	list	

Read

Easy does it as you read one small section at a time. Reading is like being at a buffet. The words go down more easily if you slow down, chew thoroughly, and remember that you can always go back for more. Active eating usually involves using a utensil, such as a knife, fork, spoon, or chopsticks. Similarly, when reading a textbook, use a pen, pencil, or highlighter to mark key words on the page as you digest the information. Read selectively. You do not need to read every word in order to get the main ideas.

Here are several reading shortcuts that can help you to "digest" the important information:

- Highlight, underline, write in the margin of the text or in your notebook. It is effective to highlight the most important words in a paragraph, rather than highlighting entire sentences or paragraphs.
- Find the core of each sentence by locating the subject-verb-object structure.
- Read the first two sentences of each paragraph to find the topic sentence. Then scan the rest of the paragraph to see how the main idea is developed.
- Paraphrase the main idea of each paragraph.
- Pretend to question the author about what he or she has written. Read to find the answer.
- Scan the paragraph for reference to a diagram or illustration. Studying captions and visual graphics can clarify information.
- Ask questions in the margins of the text.
- Reread to find answers to your questions.
- Note any unanswered questions to bring to class.
- Make flash cards.
- Associate ideas with what you already know.

Recite

After you have actively read a section, close the book and recite what you remember. Jot down what you remembered. Then check your memory against the text. Copy down the areas of information that you did not remember and concentrate on that information. Study the information in small units and take frequent short breaks so your mind can process each section thoroughly. Be sure to seek to understand the material, not just to cover the pages.

Review

After you have successfully recited each section, blend all the steps into one major process. Use your notes to test yourself on all the material you have read. Review the material until you think you can explain all the important ideas to someone else. Reward yourself for your success. This is a good time to get together with another classmate or two and explain the information to one another, ask questions, and clarify concepts. In looking for someone with whom to study, you need not select the so-called smartest people in the class. Valuable study time may be shared among students who are serious about succeeding, regardless of their grade point average. Usually what one student does not understand, another will be able to explain. By explaining concepts to one another, students solidify their own understanding and increase their own comprehension. Cramming the night before a test is usually counterproductive. Do a little each day, and you will find that what you learn becomes embedded in your mind.

■ TIPS FOR SUCCESS ■
Taking Notes

1. At the start of a lecture, be ready to take down information and jot down questions that come to mind.
2. Pick up clues by listening for key words, tone of voice, and repetition of key concepts.
3. Ask for clarification if you don't understand something.
4. Use the Cornell note-taking system or the SQ3R study method.
5. Survey each chapter of a reading assignment to get a sense of the big picture. Look at chapter titles as well as large print, boldface, and italicized headings. Survey the illustrations, diagrams, and drawings.
6. Ask focused questions as you read.
7. Use a pen, pencil, or highlighter to flag important words and ideas as you digest the information.
8. After you have actively read and understood a section, close the book and recite what you remember from memory.
9. Get together with another classmate or two or organize a study group to explain information to one another, ask questions, and clarify concepts.
10. Ask the professor if you are allowed to bring a tape recorder to class. While you jot notes in class, you can also record the information and review it later to pick up points you missed.
11. Experiment with taking notes by hand on paper or a Tablet PC, using a laptop computer, or using some other electronic device such as a personal digital assistant (PDA) to see what works best for you.

SCENARIO FOR SUCCESS

Michael Stein always seems to have problems taking notes in his psychology class. The instructor speaks very quickly, and Michael often misses out on large chunks of material from the class lectures while he is so busy writing everything down. Reading assignments in the class often cover several chapters, and Michael is falling behind. After the first two weeks of class, he decides to go to the learning center on campus and meet with a tutor to discuss ways of taking efficient notes.

Michael took several steps to improve his note-taking skills. First, he bought a three-ring binder with a supply of loose-leaf paper and used dividers to create sections for each class. Second, he began to use the same note-taking format for his lecture notes and his reading assignment notes. Third, after talking to other students in the class who were having trouble with taking notes, he organized a study group to share notes, reflect on them, and prepare for tests.

In a short time, Michael's confidence was restored, and he became so adept at his new system of taking notes that he was hired by the learning center to tutor other students. He also formed lasting friendships with some of the members of his study group, which improved his social life.

Questions for Discussion

1. What experiences have you had that are similar to Michael's experience in the case above?
2. What note-taking techniques have you developed that have enabled you to be successful? Share them with your classmates.
3. Which of the tips for success listed above have you found useful in taking notes?
4. What do you see yourself doing differently to improve your ability to take notes?

ACTIVITIES FOR SUCCESS

Activity 1: Taking Notes During Lectures

Objective: To improve your note-taking skills during lectures.

Procedure: In groups of three or four students, share your experience of using the Cornell note-taking system during one of the lectures in this course. If your instructor does not use the lecture format, form groups of three or four students from the class who are taking another course together.

Step 1: After you have formed groups, prepare your 8½ × 11 inch sheets of paper formatted for the Cornell system. (See page 38 for an illustration of the format.)

Step 2: Decide which course you will use to practice the Cornell system.

Step 3: Set a date for sharing notes with your group.

Step 4: Discuss what worked well for you in the system and what did not work well.

Activity 2: Taking Notes While You Read

Objectives: (1) To experience note-taking techniques in reading situations; (2) to select the techniques that work best for you.

Procedure: Work with a partner.

Step 1: With a partner, select a short section of a textbook, preferably one both of you are using.

Step 2: Together, survey the selection, reading aloud the headings and looking at the illustrations.

Step 3: Individually, write two or three questions about the material. Share your questions and comment on their importance.

Step 4: Read the selection, either aloud or silently.

Step 5: Take turns reciting ideas that both of you think are important.

Step 6: Review by making a list of the ideas that you can study later at test time.

Activity 3: Taking Notes When You Listen

In developing note-taking skills, consider that writing too much can be as detrimental to study as writing too little. Practicing new techniques can help you strike a balance.

Objectives: (1) To experience note-taking techniques for a variety of situations; (2) to select the techniques that fit your preferred learning style (see Chapter 5).

Procedure: Work with a partner.

Step 1: Watch a college lecture that has been presented on cable or public television. Take notes as you watch and listen. If this activity is done during class, compare your notes with those of your classmates. By reviewing the notes with others, you will increase your effectiveness in taking notes. If it is not during class, make arrangements with a classmate to compare notes.

Step 2: Ask another student to interview you about a personal topic of your choice. The topic might be your family, your career goal, or a sport you enjoy. The other student will ask you questions and take notes on the information you provide. Then you will interview that student. When it is your turn to be the reporter, take thorough notes. Quote the person directly when appropriate. Then compile the notes into coherent form and read them back to the other person. How accurate were you? If you misunderstood information, try to figure out why.

Step 3: Discuss with your partner the note-taking methods that worked well for each of you.

Step 4: Either in writing or in a discussion with your partner, review how your preferred note-taking methods correspond to your preferred learning style. Suggest ways you might change your methods to become more effective at taking notes.

JOURNAL FOR SUCCESS

Journal Entry

Objective: To reflect upon the changes in the way you study and retain knowledge based on new note-taking techniques.

Procedure: After doing at least one of the three activities in this chapter, reflect upon the results and the implications for you in terms of future situations when taking notes effectively will be advantageous to you.

CHAPTER 8

Successful Learning from Textbooks

All that mankind has done, thought, gained, or been: it is lying as in magic preservation in the pages of books.

—Thomas Carlyle

To Learn and Understand

- How can you determine the message in what you read?
- What techniques can you use to make your study time more effective?
- How can you build your word usage and understanding?

8.1 UNDERSTANDING THE CONTENT

When you first begin to use a textbook, it is wise to do an **overview** of the book—go through all of it and begin to understand its structure and resources. Most textbooks use similar structures to guide readers through the content. You are probably familiar with most of them from high school. These are the most common features:

1. *Table of contents:* This section, found at the front of textbooks, gives a detailed listing of headings that are in the book and the pages on which to find them.
2. *Chapters:* The content is usually subdivided into chapters, each of which focuses your attention on a particular aspect of the subject of the book.
3. *Glossary:* This section is usually at the end of a textbook, and it is similar to a mini-dictionary. It provides the definition for key terms found in the book. Often these terms appear throughout the text in boldface or italic font.
4. *Citations/bibliography:* Other material that has been published about the subject of a textbook may be quoted throughout the book. Each of the original sources of these quotes is listed in a reference/bibliography section at the end of a chapter or at the back of the book.
5. *Index:* This is usually the final section of the book. It provides the reader with a series of **cross references**— a way of looking up the page number for most concepts and key subjects found throughout the book.

The Content

Before reading a section or chapter of a textbook, you can get the big picture by using a technique called **scanning**. Look over the whole section and make sure you observe the format. Scan the words by glancing over them to get a general sense of the main information points you will need to understand.

Understanding the words themselves, however, is even more critical. Throughout your higher education years, you will read unfamiliar words. In some cases, you can determine the meaning from the **context**—the whole sentence or paragraph around a word. However, in many instances, the best action to take is to look the word up in the glossary at the back of the book or in a dictionary. You may find it helpful to maintain a vocabulary journal of the new words you are learning so you can practice using them.

Author's Intended Message (AIM)

We all want to be understood. Authors in particular write in such a way that the reader will understand them and will be able to find the **author's intended message (AIM)**. There are several keys that can unlock the AIM, intentionally planted by the author to make the message clear:

1. Title
2. Chapter and unit headings
3. Topic sentence and supporting details

Title   Obviously, in textbooks, the title of a book or chapter is a clear indicator of the AIM. Often a writer will use the title to create interest as well as to inform. Each book needs a title that provides an overview of the author's AIM. Consider these examples:

AIM: To help readers realize their inner potential.
TITLE: *Revolution from Within*

AIM: To make one a better writer
TITLE: *Handbook for Writers*

Chapter and Unit Headings   Authors provide chapter and unit headings that clearly show the reader what topic is under discussion. By providing these headings, the author simplifies the management of a great deal of information, making it easier for the reader to locate the information needed.

For example, an author writing about the broad topic of "television" might use a variety of methods to organize the text:

I.   Definition of television (definition)
II. History of development of television (chronology)
III. Technology of television (facts)
IV. Effects of television on society (cause-effect; statistics)

Topic Sentence and Supporting Details   Ordinarily, authors place the topic sentence first in the paragraph to help the reader gain an overview of the paragraph. Sometimes, however, the topic sentence may be in the middle or at the end of the paragraph. In the paragraph below, the topic sentence, which is underlined, is located at the end of the paragraph, providing the reader with a synthesis of the details. The details that support the topic sentence are examples. Other ways to support the topic sentence are through classification (a listing of key parts), reasons, cause-effect, story (anecdote), facts, and definition.

> Designers are creating fabrics that reflect diversity, individuality, and harmony with the environment. Unique handmade clothing illustrates the influence of the Southwest and Native American cultures through use of beads, leather, and hand-woven cottons. Patchwork designs from Guatemala create sparkling color combinations for a bold and earthy look. Moroccan and Balinese patterns accent rayon moon and stars patterns. Unique hand-embroidered designs of chickens, monkeys, and deer make children's T-shirts delightful and dressy. <u>Creating designs and fabrics drawn from renewable resources is one of many ways in which artists are raising the consciousness of consumers.</u>

8.2 UNDERSTANDING VISUAL CONTENT

Graphs, diagrams, charts, and illustrations enhance the textbook presentation and are usually easier to assimilate than an explanation in words only, because they engage different learning styles and improve the likelihood of remembering the material. By developing critical questions before reading the chapter, you can jump-start your learning process so that when you do a close reading of the information, the visuals will support your understanding.

To fully understand the content of a textbook, you must use all of your powers of observation. Textbooks often contain illustrations, graphics, charts, summary notes in the margins, and highlighted word definitions. Figures 8.A and 8.B are examples of illustrations for different types of content.

Bar Graph

A **bar graph** generally provides a visual depiction of statistical data to make the data easier to understand. Interpreting a bar graph requires that you understand what each element in the graph represents. In the example provided, Figure 8.1, note the following:

- The graph has five columns, which correspond to the five academic years covered in the study.
- In each column are four differentiated bars, each representing a specific source of student financial aid.
- Below the graph are boxes that show what source of aid each type of bar represents.
- To the left of the graph are figures ranging from 0 to 22, representing millions of dollars. For example, in the first column, 1997–98, the tallest bar falls between the numbers 12 and 14. This shows that John Carroll grants and scholarships accounted for almost 13 million dollars in financial aid to students that year.

1. What was the approximate increase in federal-sponsored loans (self-help) between the 1999–2000 and 2001–2002 academic years?
2. What was the approximate increase in student aid in the form of university grants and scholarships during the same period?
3. Which source of funding increased the least between the 2000–2001 and 2001–2002 academic years?

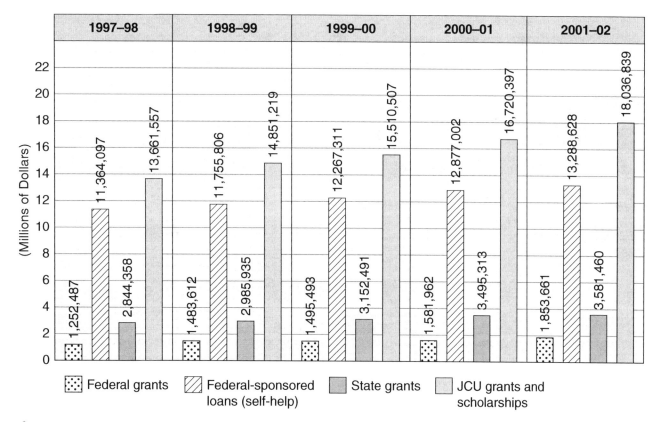

Figure 8.1 ▪ Financial Aid to John Carroll Students (1997–98 – 2001–02). The bar graph depicts shares of financial aid provided to John Carroll students from four sources.

Reprinted by permission of John Carroll University, University Heights, Ohio

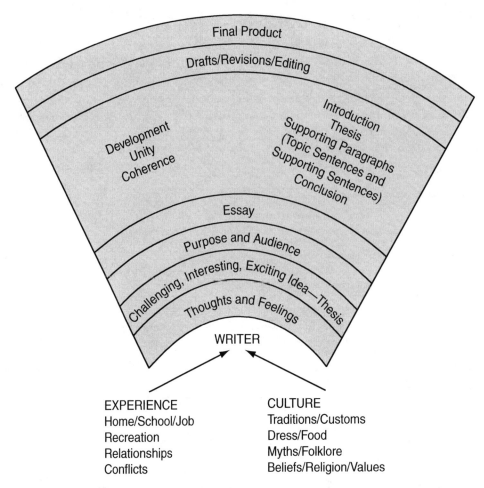

Figure 8.2 ■ Example of an Illustration. This illustration demonstrates the essay-writing process.
Used with permission, George Eppley and Anita Dixon Eppley

Illustration

Figure 8.2 is an example of an illustration from a textbook. Illustrations provide concrete expression of concepts discussed in the book.

1. Describe the illustration in detail.
2. What is its function?
3. How does it contribute to your understanding of the writing process?

8.3 CONCENTRATION TECHNIQUES

It's very easy for your mind to wander when you are studying. There can be nearly endless distractions and diversions that take you away from your purpose. You will find it helpful to develop the skill of **concentration**—intense focus on the matter at hand—so that your study time is effective. Here are some helpful techniques:

- Remember why you are studying: not just to pass a test but to be effective, competent, and confident.
- Study at the natural learning peak time for you—early morning, after a nap, before/after a meal, late at night. If you are not sure when your natural learning peak time is, experiment until you find it.
- If possible, study outside the home so that you are not distracted by telephone, television, family, friends, and other projects.
- Set a specific, measurable study goal that can be accomplished in a specific amount of time.
- Take a few moments to breathe deeply before beginning to study.
- If you have difficulty concentrating on one subject, leave it for a short time and study another subject.

Figure 8.3 ▪ Ruby-throated Hummingbird

- Keep your hand and mind busy by jotting down questions as you study, **annotating** a section you are reading by underlining, highlighting, and making notes in the margins, or making an outline as a study aid (see below).
- Promise yourself a little reward if you use your study time well and successfully.

8.4 CREATING STUDY AIDS

Study aids can enhance your study skills capability. These may include making a timeline, outline, map, or process diagram, or annotating text. These techniques help you connect ideas in the text in different ways.

Read the following information from the Website of the Texas Environmental Studies Institute at Rice University about the migratory habits of ruby-throated hummingbirds:

> Ruby-throated hummingbirds, *archilochus colubris*, migrate through Texas in the fall months heading for balmy Mexico. This migration extends from the eastern two-thirds of Texas from September to December and March to May as far west as the Pecos River and the Panhandle of Texas. They breed in summer east of the Edwards Plateau from the Red River to the Central Coast. Male ruby-throated hummingbirds migrate before the females back to Mexico. During the fall migration, the birds fly across Texas moving between 25 to 30 miles per hour. Some migrants fly nonstop across the Gulf of Mexico while some move inland down the Texas coast.

Figure 8.3 above is an illustration showing what a ruby-throated hummingbird looks like.

Timeline

A timeline helps you to place information in a meaningful order according to chronological events. Using the information on the ruby-throated hummingbirds, you can create a timeline that provides you with a visual tool that can help you remember the migratory habits of the birds throughout the year. Here in Figure 8.4 is an example of a timeline:

Migration across Eastern Texas	Migration to Pecos River and Panhandle	Breeding east of Edwards Plateau
September–December	March–May	Summer

Figure 8.4 ▪ Example of a Timeline

Outline

Creating an outline of the information is another way to study the migratory pattern of the ruby-throated hummingbirds:

I. Fall migration: September–December
   A. Destination is Mexico
   B. Migration begins in eastern two-thirds of Texas

II. Spring migration: March–May
   A. Migration west to Pecos River
   B. Migration to Panhandle of Texas

III. Summer breeding
   A. East of the Edwards Plateau from the Red River to the Central Coast
   B. Males migrate before females back to Mexico

IV. Speeds and destinations
   A. During fall migration, 25–30 miles per hour
   B. Some fly nonstop across Gulf of Mexico
   C. Some move inland down Texas coast

Map

Mapping the direction of the migration is another creative way to study the migratory pattern of ruby-throated hummingbirds, particularly if your learning style is visual (see the discussion on learning styles in Chapter 5).

Below is an example of a map:

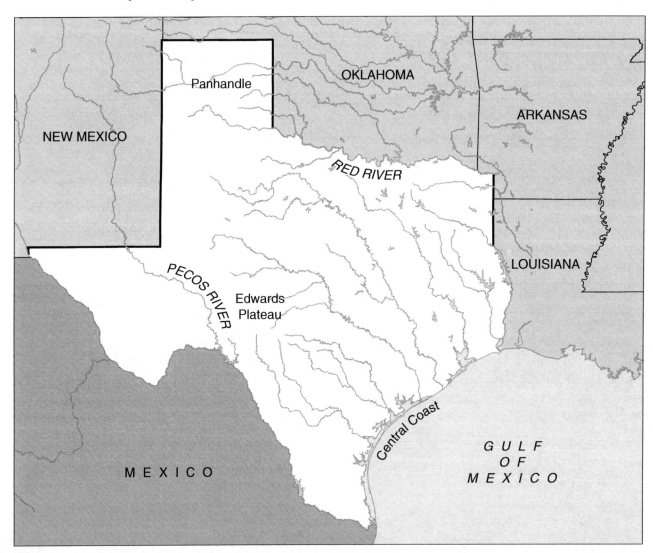

Figure 8.5 ■ Map of Texas

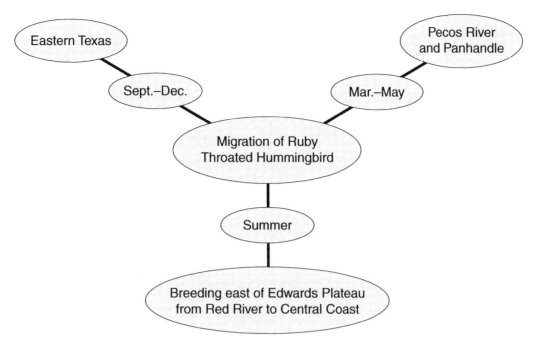

Figure 8.6 ■ Example of a Process Diagram

Process Diagram
To connect the various phases of the migratory process of ruby-throated hummingbirds, create a process diagram like the one shown in Figure 8.6.

Annotation
Another way to help you remember information is to annotate the text. You will find your annotations particularly helpful later in the semester when you are preparing for a test. Figure 8.7 illustrates an annotated selection on the migratory process of ruby-throated hummingbirds:

migrate in fall	Ruby-throated hummingbirds, *archilochus colubris*, migrate through Texas in the fall months heading for balmy Mexico.	*head for Mexico*
	This migration extends from the eastern two-thirds of Texas from September to	*Sept. to Dec. from E. Tex.*
March to May—west to Pecos R & Panhandle	December and March to May as far west as the Pecos River and the Panhandle of Texas. They breed in	*breeding time*
	summer east of the Edwards Plateau from the Red River to the Central	
guys before gals to Mex.	Coast. Male ruby-throated hummingbirds migrate before the females back to Mexico. During the fall migration, the birds fly across Texas moving between	
speed	25 to 30 miles per hour. Some migrants fly nonstop across the Gulf of Mexico while some move inland down the Texas coast.	

Figure 8.7 ■ Example of an Annotated Selection

■ TIPS FOR SUCCESS ■
Learning from Textbooks

1. Read with concentration, giving your best attention and focus.
2. Create a "reading area" that is conducive to maximizing efficient reading. For example, if you read at your desk, remove any visual distractions (such as piles of paper, books, and other projects you are working on) so you can devote your attention to your reading.
3. Take a break when you start to feel weary and are no longer absorbing the material.
4. Limit the amount of TV, movies, and video games you include in your life.
5. Keep a dictionary handy when you are reading, and look up words you don't understand. Where possible, underline the word and write down the meaning in the margin to reinforce your understanding.
6. Make a point to use at least one new word each day in your conversations.
7. Share your experience, understanding, and insights of what you are reading with others. Ask them to do the same thing with you.

SCENARIO FOR SUCCESS

Jim Scarlucci is the new sales associate for Dresher Chemical Company. He has some understanding about the chemical industry, but much of the terminology is unfamiliar. Each week he collects industry magazines from around his office and reads them in detail. He keeps a small pad of paper handy while he is reading and makes a note of each word he doesn't understand. He then looks up the words in the regular dictionary or a specialty chemical reference book to better understand the terminology. If he cannot find the information, he asks his sales manager for help in learning it. This both expands his knowledge and builds a stronger relationship with his manager.

Questions for Discussion

1. What methods have you been using to improve your reading for success?
2. What new words have you introduced recently into your vocabulary?
3. What have you done to demonstrate how you have used them in sentences?
4. Can you think of three words that others have used or you have seen in print that are new to you? Demonstrate how you might use each of these in a sentence.

ACTIVITIES FOR SUCCESS

Activity 1: Improving Study Skills

This activity is designed to introduce you to a successful study method. The more you use the method, the more proficient you will become.

Objective: To learn an improved method of studying.
Procedure:
Step 1: Before/outside class, choose a textbook you are using in another class.
Step 2: Identify a chapter of the text to study.
Step 3: Silently and alone, study your key section. Take notes on what you read by doing the following:
1. Identify the major point of the chapter.
2. List examples that illustrate this point.
3. Summarize the main points of the chapter using the headings and subheadings.
4. Select three or four related facts, then ask a question that incorporates information from those facts.

5. Refer to the end of the chapter, where textbook authors often provide a summary of important information. Select one paragraph of summary information. Give an example that illustrates the summary.

6. Using one important concept from the chapter, think of as many implications of that concept as you can.

7. When you have completed study of the section, close your book and put away your notes. Recite in your mind what you remember. Return to the text to compare what you remember with what you studied. Review the material again. If necessary, go back a third time to pick up any important information that you did not remember. This recitation process is the core of the study. If you prefer, you can write down what you remember each time.

Step 4: After you have completed the introductory activity, come to class ready to discuss the following questions as a group and to help you identify your most effective study method.

1. How did you know what section was important to choose?
2. What questions did you ask yourself?
3. What methods of taking notes did you use while reading?
4. Approximately what percentage of the information did you remember the first time you recited?
5. How did you remember this information?
6. What percentage of the information did you remember the second time you recited?
7. What helped you remember this information the second time?
8. What methods of taking notes would you use again?

Activity 2: Reading Comprehension

The following steps give you practice in strategies designed to improve reading comprehension.

Objectives: (1) To utilize strategies for improving comprehension based on a specific type of reading; (2) to gain skill in identifying examples of various types of reading.

Procedure:

Step 1: Bring to class a set of directions such as those for assembling a toy, designing a knitting or crocheting pattern, or performing an activity you enjoy.

Step 2: Explain to members of your group how you would proceed in implementing the directions.

Step 3: Then actually do a portion of the project to see whether your understanding of the directions is accurate.

Activity 3: Practicing Concentration

Objective: To learn how annotation can improve your concentration and memory.

Procedure:

Step 1: Skim the selection below.

Step 2: Write margin notes that highlight the key points in the text and that would be helpful to you in reviewing the information later.

Step 3: Compare and discuss your margin notes with those of other students.

Ernest Gaines, the award-winning novelist of *The Autobiography of Miss Jane Pittman,* is also well known for his novel, *A Lesson Before Dying,* set in rural Louisiana in the late 1940s when segregation still ruled the Deep South. This is the story of a young illiterate black man who was in the wrong place at the wrong time, condemned by a white jury to death in the electric chair for a murder he did not commit. The theme that Gaines chooses to focus on is not the injustice of this decision, but rather the question of how the protagonist, Jefferson, deals with his fate. In an effort to play on the sympathy of the jury, Jefferson's white lawyer had compared slaughtering him to slaughtering a hog. This offensive comparison prompts Jefferson's aunt to call upon the local black teacher, Grant Wiggins, to guide Jefferson to face his death with dignity and to represent the black community with pride. The novel epitomizes Gaines' ability to characterize with poignant clarity and to suggest with subtle detail an evolving growth on the part of both black young men as they assume the redemptive roles of models in their depressed, culturally deprived, segregated environments.

Activity 4: Practicing Scanning

Objective: To understand how scanning material before reading it can help you learn the material better.

Procedure: Work in pairs.

Step 1: Choose a textbook from one of your other classes and turn to a specific chapter.

Step 2: Scan the chapter to find key points.

Step 3: Share the points with a partner. Here are two examples you might choose:

Chemistry: Scan the periodic table for specific elements.

World Civilizations: Scan the world timeline to determine similarities and differences in cultures during the same time. For example, when it is 9 A.M. in Cleveland, Ohio, U.S.A., what time is it in Shanghai, China; Paris, France; or some other city? Think about what residents of each city are likely to be doing at that particular moment.

Activity 5: Practicing Summarizing

Objective: To learn the skill of identifying and communicating the essence of a verbal or written communication.

Procedure: Work in pairs.

Step 1: Taking turns, describe to another classmate an achievement that you have had in your life. Talk about the achievement for at least two minutes (time yourself).

Step 2: After you have finished describing your achievement, your partner will create a core sentence or two that captures the essential facts of what you said.

Activity 6: Improving Study Skills

Using critical thinking during studying improves effectiveness in assignments and taking tests.

Objectives: (1) To read a graph, chart, and an illustration with intelligence and understanding of the implications; (2) to look at obvious information, closely "reading" the hidden motivation or causes.

Procedure:

Step 1: Bring to class an example of a graph, chart, and illustration from a textbook.

Step 2: Using your examples, analyze at least one of each type of visual graphic. What information does it show?

Step 3: As a group, discuss how the information shown is meaningful and useful.

Step 4: Discuss what critical thinking questions your group used in order to reach a conclusion.

Activity 7: Meaning from Context

There is a certain amount of subjectivity to using language. That is why it is important to become sensitive to language usage. Your college instructors will expect you to have a familiarity with appropriate word usage.

Objective: To surmise the meaning of a word from context clues.

Procedure:

Step 1: Use context clues to make an intelligent guess as to the meaning of the underlined word in each sentence below.

Step 2: Explain the reason for your choice.

1. Having dressed for the party, Joan looked at herself in the mirror, feeling confident that her newly bought <u>habiliments</u> were appropriate for the occasion and that she would enjoy her date with Bill.

2. At the party, Bill, intending to be funny, made an unpleasant, <u>caustic</u> remark about Joan's brother Jerry's beliefs.

3. Thinking about it later, <u>incredulous</u> that Bill had been so insensitive, Joan decided to talk to him about it.

Activity 8: Meaning from Structure

Words are complex creations that sometimes seem to have little sense. However, many are structured with consistency, and understanding the structure can help you figure out their meanings.

Objective: To relate the meaning of words with their roots, prefixes, and suffixes.

Procedure:

Step 1: Discover the meaning of words by breaking them down and looking at their roots. Many of the following roots come from Latin. List several words that are derived from the root:

bio (life) _____

agri (field) _____

dorm (sleep) _____

flect, flex (bend) _____

dent (tooth) _____

Step 2: Discover the meaning of words by breaking them down and looking at their prefixes. List several related words for the prefixes below:

anti (against) _____

e, ec, ex (from, out of) _____

mal (bad, ill) _____

uni (one) _____

neo (new) _____

Step 3: Discover the meaning of words by breaking them down and looking at their suffixes. Form several related words for each suffix below:

ist _____

s, es _____

ness _____

tion _____

ish _____

Activity 9: Building Vocabulary

Knowing the meanings of prefixes, root words, and suffixes enables you to expand your store of word-tools by deciphering unfamiliar words.

Objectives: (1) To be able to identify the meanings of common prefixes, root words, and suffixes; (2) to provide basic definitions, using word clues.

Procedure:

Step 1: Create a word using the given prefixes, suffixes, and roots.

Prefix	Meaning	Create a Word
ad	to, toward	*advance*
ante	before	
anti	against	
de	down	
in, il	not	
non, un	not	
inter	between	
trans	across	
mono	one	
semi	half	
sub	under	
super	over, above	
pro	for	
contra	against	

Suffix	Meaning	Create a Word
ate	to make	*create*
able	capable of being	
an	person who	
ant	person who	
ar	relating to	
ary	place where	
en	made of	
ence	state or quality	
fy	to make	

Suffix	Meaning	Create a Word
hood	state or condition	_____
ible	capable of being	_____
ic	like or made of	_____
less	without	_____
ment	state of being	_____
or	person who	_____
ous	abounding in	_____
some	tending to	_____
ward	direction, course	_____

Roots	Meaning	Create a Word
aqua	water	*aquarium*
audio	hear	_____
bene	well	_____
cor, cord	heart	_____
corp	body	_____
cred	belief	_____
ego	self	_____
frater	brother	_____
mit, mis	end	_____
pos	place	_____
script	write	_____
sol	alone	_____
vid, vis	see	_____
auto	self	_____
bio	life	_____
geo	earth	_____
graphy	write	_____
log	speech, science	_____
pseud	false	_____
tele	far	_____

Step 2: After you have reviewed the list of prefixes, roots, and suffixes, use the following activity to test yourself.

Match the word with its basic meaning. Give attention to the word clues in making your decision.

1. transmit
2. urbaphobia
3. monarchy
4. bibliophile
5. antebellum
6. endoskeleton
7. amoral
8. microscopic
9. transition
10. Anglophile
11. transcontinental
12. contradict
13. occupant
14. cordial
15. solitude

a. before the war
b. one ruler
c. very small
d. fear of cities
e. without morals
f. one who loves books
g. send across
h. inner skeleton
i. one who loves England
j. a change
k. from the heart
l. going across countries
m. person who lives in a place
n. speak against
o. alone

Journal Entry

Objective: To apply and learn from the benefits of practicing the tips for success in this chapter.

Procedure: Reread the tips for success on page 50. Choose two or three and integrate them into your study practices for one week. Then reflect and write about the results of these new behaviors.

CHAPTER 9

Taking Tests Successfully

Welcome every problem as an opportunity. Each moment is the great challenge, the best thing that ever happened to you. The more difficult the problem, the greater the challenge in working it out.

—Grace Speare

To Learn and Understand

- How do you prepare yourself for taking tests?
- What skills are needed for taking tests?
- How can you remember information better?
- What if you are tempted to cheat?

9.1 PREPARATION

Even hearing the word "test" can start a stress response in most people. The past might instantly intrude in the form of memories of difficult high school tests. Tests and examinations are an integral part of college, however, so it's important to learn how to be successful with them. Tests may be an ongoing part of your career as well. Many professions require you to take continuing education course work and tests to maintain your professional license and credentials. Some companies also offer training classes that include tests.

Changing Your Thoughts

The first step toward success in taking tests is to change your thoughts about tests. Instead of thinking that tests are events to be avoided, see them as opportunities to demonstrate how much you know. Successful students often picture exams as the big game in which they get the chance to prove they belong among the best performers. Such thoughts drive out the fear of exams and motivate you to study and to excel.

Study Methods

The second step involves study methods: how to study, how to prepare for the big game. Psychologist and lecturer Martin Schuster has reinforced what students have long known: Too much study at one time is counterproductive. In *Learning to Learn,* written in collaboration with Werner Metzig, Schuster advises students not to study more than six to eight hours a day, interspersing that study time with a nap between sessions. Okay, so six to eight hours a day might sound a little excessive to you. Think of it as a full-time job, where you will be expected to work eight hours a day. Moreover, when it comes time to prepare for final exams, suddenly it will seem as if there aren't enough study hours in the day.

Study Location

Schuster also suggests changes of scenery while you study. One day, the library might work best. Another day, a nearby hill or grassy area could beckon. Sometimes a dorm room or even your car is a quiet spot. Another time, you might be more productive with fellow classmates in a common area. Experiment to find what works best for you and be aware of your need to shift places if you are becoming tired or losing concentration.

The RAT Formula

A three-step method of handling the stress related to taking tests that reinforces Schuster's findings is the "RAT" formula. It can be summarized in just a few words:

- **R**elaxation
- **A**nticipation
- **T**esting skills

Relaxation   As you enter the room where you will take the test, it is important to let go of tension. A simple relaxation technique is a deep-breathing exercise such as the following: Count backward from 100 or say "1, 2, 3—I'm breathing in peace; 4, 5, 6—I'm breathing out fear." An alternative to deep breathing is progressive muscle relaxation: Actively tense and relax each major muscle group in your body, proceeding from toes to head and back again several times.

Self-talk—thinking positive thoughts in order to displace distractions and negative messages—is another effective way to release anxiety. When you combine self-talk with visualization or a positive imaging of results, you will become less sensitive to anxious feelings. Every day during the semester say to yourself, "I am an excellent student studying very hard and learning everything I need to know to successfully pass all my exams." While taking tests, repeat to yourself, "I am doing my best, and I will get an excellent grade." At the same time, you might picture yourself writing the correct answers and the instructor placing a high grade on your paper.

Schuster found that using positive language in self-talk makes a significant difference. One of his female clients told herself every morning, "I won't fail. I won't fail," and promptly did poorly in her exam. "The negative word 'fail' stuck in her mind," Schuster said. "If she had used a positive phrase like 'I'll pass,' she would have made it through the exam."

Another relaxation technique Schuster advocates is mentally recalling a time in your life when you were successful. Picture yourself in that situation again and identify the positive feelings you had.

Relaxing includes eating well and having sufficient rest before taking the test. Wear comfortable clothing, and choose a seat that enables you to relax with few distractions. Leave other concerns outside the classroom door. If you are mentally and physically relaxed, you are likely to be alert and feel more confident.

Anticipation   Anticipate what the test will cover. If you are not sure about the format of the test, ask the professor a few days before so that you can prepare. Sometimes a professor will suggest that you purchase a workbook that accompanies the text. You might have second thoughts about the purchase, especially if money is not readily available. Usually, however, the purchase is well worth the sacrifice. Teachers who make such recommendations frequently use actual questions from the workbook for their tests.

If the test will have objective questions—including true-false, matching, completion, or multiple choice—you will need to be prepared to give dates, facts, and definitions. For a subjective test including essays, you will need to prepare by answering comprehensive questions.

It is important to know how significant the test will be in determining your final grade so that you can gauge how much time you need to prepare. The best way to do well at any test is by being thoroughly prepared.

Testing Skills   Here are some suggestions about different types of test questions that can help you answer the questions more accurately.

True-False Questions   Read every word in the statement. Words in the statement that allow for exceptions, such as *sometimes, generally,* and *usually* are more likely to be true. If any one part of the statement is false, mark it false. The word *always* is frequently an indicator that the statement is false. Ask how the test will be scored to know if you will be rewarded or penalized for guessing.

Examples

1. Research suggests that companies generally need both leadership and strong management in order to be successful.

   Answer: True

2. Transactional leaders guide their followers in the direction of established goals by clarifying role and task requirements and by creating realistic, credible, and attractive visions.

   Answer: False

   Explanation: The first part of the statement is true of transactional leaders, but creating realistic, credible, and attractive visions more accurately describes visionary leaders.

Multiple-Choice Questions These questions require that you recognize the correct answer from a group. Eliminate the ones you know right away are incorrect. Frequently, the longest answer is the correct answer. "All of the above" is often correct, while "none of the above" is usually incorrect. When two statements are opposite, one of them is usually the correct answer.

Do all the questions on the test you know first, checking or circling the numbers of the ones you want to come back to later. Watch for key phrases like, "Choose the one that *best* fits." Be aware of decoy answers that were not covered in class or in the textbook; these are usually incorrect.

Examples

1. Which of the following best indicates the goal of future graduates?
   a. They seek a salary of at least $30,000 a year.
   b. They look for a competitive and challenging work environment.
   c. They seek opportunities for advancement and autonomy in the job.
   d. All of the above are correct.
   e. None of the above are correct.

   Answer: d

2. Gain-sharing seems to fit current conditions better than piece-rate reward systems because
   a. Gain-sharing affects production employees and support people only.
   b. Most of the time gain-sharing does not meet the needs of organizations for increased productivity.
   c. Most of the time gain-sharing is developed and administered in a participative fashion, requiring less administrative support and rewarding both the organization and each individual.
   d. Both (b) and (c).

   Answer: c

   Explanation: Not only is (c) a longer answer, but it is also opposite of (b).

Short-Answer Questions In short-answer questions, you need to be skillful in following directions, putting the answer in the right space, and spelling words and terms related to the subject correctly. Check to be sure that you are actually providing the information that is asked.

Example

What are the qualities of a tragic hero according to Aristotle?

Answer: Aristotle believed that the tragic hero or protagonist in a Greek tragedy had to be a man of noble birth who was a positive leader in many respects but who had one character defect or tragic flaw. Allowing this flaw to influence his actions and cause his downfall was called "hubris" in Greek, meaning "pride" or "arrogance."

Explanation: In this response, the student brings together the terms associated with the tragic hero: *protagonist, noble birth, tragic flaw.* The answer is brief and to the point.

Matching Questions In matching questions, read all the items and mark the easiest and most obvious ones first. Cross off extra items that do not seem to have a match before pairing items that fit together. Be aware of matching items by association. For example, a biology instructor may have referred to dendrites as looking like spider webs. On a test, the instructor may match those items, assuming that you have listened carefully to the lecture.

Example

Select the definition in column B that *best* defines the word in column A. Place the letter from the column B answer in the blank next to the word.

Column A	Column B
1. coexisting __c__	**a.** to live together
2. antagonist __e__	**b.** to say again
3. consternation __g__	**c.** getting along with others
4. accelerate __f__	**d.** to slow down
5. reiterate __b__	**e.** one who is in conflict with another
	f. to speed up
	g. confusion

Explanation:

1. *Coexisting* has the prefix co-, meaning "with" and the suffix -ing. The definition "getting along with others" matches the prefix and the suffix.
2. *Antagonist* has a form of the prefix anti-, meaning "against" and the suffix -ist, meaning "one who."
3. *Consternation* has the prefix con-, meaning "with" and the suffix -ion, indicating a noun.
4. *Accelerate* has the root cel- meaning "swift" and the suffix -ate, indicating a verb.
5. *Reiterate* has the prefix re-, which means "again," and the suffix -ate, which indicates a verb form.

Essay Tests You will need to provide different types of information and content for essay tests. Read all the questions before beginning to prepare your answer. If you have options, choose the one that is easiest for you. The key verb, called the *prompt verb,* in the essay instructions will guide you in how to organize your answer. You may find it helpful to quickly outline your answer on a piece of scrap paper before starting to write. Here are some prompt verbs that are used in essay questions:

prove	Show by argument or logic that it is true.
define	Give the formal meaning by distinguishing it from related terms.
justify	State why you think it is so.
compare	Show similarities and differences.
illustrate	Explain or make clear by concrete examples, comparisons, or analogies.
synthesize	Show the connections between things, telling how one causes the other.
discuss	Describe and explain the pros and cons.
summarize	Give a brief account of the main ideas; omit details and examples.
analyze	Find the main ideas, and show how they are related and why they are important.

9.2 MEMORY TOOLS

Understanding is the key that unlocks associations that can be helpful in memorizing information, rather than just using rote drilling. Before attempting to memorize information, seek to understand it. Humor helps the brain to remember content more easily, so incorporate a little humor where you can. Some of the following techniques may be helpful to you:

- Overlearn.
- Put information to use right away.

- Visualize where on a page the information is located and what titles and subtitles are near it.
- Create a metaphor that makes sense to you.
- Record and play back your notes.
- Study with a team or at least another person.
- Make flash cards.
- Review information just before you go to sleep.
- Review and correct class material as soon as possible after the class ends.
- Associate information with people, funny incidents, or examples.
- If your course work involves learning physical concepts, such as parts of the body or the DNA structure, draw the objects or mold them in clay. If your college provides manipulative models, use them to help you associate the physical model with the content.
- Use acronyms—that is, new words (real or invented) formed by combining the first letters of other words. For example, if you are trying to memorize the seven coordinating conjunctions (*for, and, nor, but, or, yet, so*), you might create the word FANBOYS (created by using the first letter of each word).
- Make up a sentence in which each word represents the initial letter of a word you need to remember. For example, the sentence *Every Good Boy Does Fine* is often used to help beginning music students remember notes on the five lines on a scale: E, G, B, D, and F.
- Picture historic events in such a way that you will remember them, perhaps with a little humor. For example, to remember that George Washington crossed the Delaware River, picture him dipping his big toe in the water and yelling, "Della! Beware!"
- Make coincidental connections. For example, to remember the name of Neil Armstrong, the American astronaut who was the first man to walk on the lunar surface, picture him in his NASA space suit, with the monogram "N.A.," coincidentally the first two letters of NASA.
- Draw events in your own unique way. For example, draw a picture of the Great Wall of China with the graffiti "Ming 15th Century" to remember when the later fortifications were begun.
- If you are an auditory learner, put the words of a concept you are memorizing to the tune of a popular commercial or song.

With increasing frequency, professors are challenging their students to go beyond the basic levels of information and comprehension to the higher-level critical-thinking questions that show up in essay questions. Tests are as individual as the professor. Learning to understand your teacher's approach and style will be helpful to you in learning and succeeding.

9.3 CHEATING

As cheating has grown to epidemic proportions, colleges have begun to take serious action to stop the practice. Professors are given guidelines for spotting and dealing with cheaters. Remember, professors can access the same Internet information that you can, and they often have special software programs to check student materials, so do not **plagiarize.** Documenting any source of information is essential in any writing that you do, whether in college or in your career. Whether you quote a source or explain an idea from a source in your own words, you must give credit to the author. If you do not, you are plagiarizing. Use a reference handbook to help you document sources accurately and correctly.

Colleges are intent on changing the culture of cheating because they recognize that ultimately it hurts the students who do it. Cheating devalues you, the others in your class, and your learning as a whole. If you are caught cheating, you could fail a class, face suspension from your school, and have a note in your permanent file. The best advice about cheating? Don't do it. It's not worth it. You are better than that!

Cheating has also become more common in the workplace, with some significant negative consequences. People have lost prestigious awards, managers have been imprisoned, and executives have been required to pay back millions of dollars to shareholders. Operating businesses with a high standard of **ethics** is even more important than maintaining your **integrity** in your college course work. People's lives are at stake.

■ TIPS FOR SUCCESS ■
Taking Tests

1. Be clear about your goals in reading all study material.
2. Apply reading success techniques whenever you are faced with large reading projects.
3. Be aware when you are experiencing information overload and need to stop for a while or change activities.
4. Apply stress-reduction practices when faced with a test.
5. Request coaching from someone who is successful at taking tests.
6. Practice taking tests.
7. Play memory games—see how long you can remember a license plate number, a phone number, a poem, or a quotation.

SCENARIO FOR SUCCESS

Shareefah Chakar is a customer service specialist for Trans-National Telephone Company. Every six months she must take a certification test on new products and services. Each day she receives packets of reference material important for her job. It's easy for her to feel overloaded with the volume of material she has to read and know. She allocates an hour each afternoon to scan and categorize the material in her reference binders. Shareefah sets aside reference material to read in the first quiet hour of the morning before frequent calls come in from customers.

Questions for Discussion

1. Do you ever experience information overload similar to that described in the above scenario? What do you do to manage the situation?
2. What tips for success have you used to improve your handling of large volumes of information in studying for exams?
3. What can you see yourself doing differently to enhance your success in taking tests?

ACTIVITIES FOR SUCCESS

Activity 1: Relaxing While Preparing for Taking Tests

Success in taking tests lies in relaxing, anticipating what you need to know, and using memory techniques to help you retain information.

Objective: To practice relaxation techniques.
Procedure: Do activities individually and with a partner.
   Step 1: Experiment on your own with the following relaxation techniques.
   1. Count backward from 100 while breathing in and out deeply. Stop when you feel relaxed.
   2. Close your eyes and visualize a scene in nature that brings you pleasure.
   3. Start with your feet and tighten and relax all the major muscle groups in your body, going upward and finishing with your head and face.
   Step 2: Find a partner and discuss techniques (1), (2), and (3) with your partner. Which techniques did each of you find helpful? Which ones can you add from your own experience?

Activity 2: Constructing a Test

This exercise is designed to give you experience in constructing a short test.

Objective: To understand how short-answer tests work.
Procedure: Work with a partner.
   Step 1: Bring a newspaper article to class.

Step 2: Construct a five-question objective quiz on the newspaper article you brought to class. Then give the article to another student, who will read and study it to remember the content. Before the student begins to read the selection, provide cues such as, "Notice the topic of this article," or "Carefully read the second paragraph." Those cues should help the student anticipate what will be on the quiz. After your partner has read the article, give him or her the quiz. Then, either reverse positions, with you being the quiz-taker, or exchange articles and study them and then take the quizzes in parallel.

Step 3: Discuss the following questions with your partner:

1. What cues did you pick up from your student "teacher"?
2. Were you able to anticipate the kinds of questions that you would be asked on the quiz? Why or why not?
3. How would you like your teacher to prepare you for an objective test?

Step 4: With your partner, rehearse how you would ask your teacher what would be on an objective test; when you would approach the teacher; and how you would ask for further clarification if you needed it.

JOURNAL FOR SUCCESS

Journal Entry

Objective: To reinforce your change of thinking toward taking tests.

Procedure:

Step 1: Reflect upon and write your thoughts about how you are changing to having a more positive and empowered attitude toward tests. How hard was it to change your thinking? What results have you observed from your efforts?

Step 2: Describe the success you have had in using the "RAT" formula.

Step 3: Indicate what memory tools you have found most helpful in preparing for tests.

CHAPTER 10

Personal Growth Success

As I interpret the Course [in Miracles], "our deepest fear is not that we are inadequate. Our deepest fear is that we are powerful beyond measure. It is our light, not our darkness, that most frightens us." We ask ourselves, Who am I to be brilliant, gorgeous, talented, fabulous? Actually, who are you not *to be? You are a child of God. Your playing small doesn't serve the world. There's nothing enlightened about shrinking so that other people won't feel insecure around you. We are all meant to shine, as children do. We were born to make manifest the glory of God that is within us. It's not just in some of us; it's in everyone. And as we let our own light shine, we unconsciously give other people permission to do the same. As we're liberated from our own fear, our presence automatically liberates others.*

—Marianne Williamson

To Learn and Understand

- What are self-esteem, self-concept, and self-confidence?
- What is your idea of personal success? How can visualization help you achieve it?
- Why is it helpful to set goals?

10.1 POSITIVE SELF-TALK, SELF-ESTEEM, AND SELF-RESPECT

Achieving personal growth begins with **self-awareness, self-assessment,** and **self-acceptance.** It involves observing your own behavior and attitudes, looking at where you are now, and accepting the stage you are at in your life. This process provides the space and freedom to look for where you want to grow and develop and enables you to set the goals to achieve your vision.

Your **values**—the principles or standards that you have been taught or have adopted to use as guides for your actions—will affect your behavior in college and at work. For example, you may have been taught to always speak respectfully to teachers. You may have a value that says, "Hard workers get ahead, so I am going to work hard." Behavior that respects the value of the environment would include recycling and picking up one's own and other people's trash and depositing it in appropriate containers.

It is important to be clear about your values as you set goals and objectives in your life. The more important a goal is to you, and the more it reflects your values, the more effort you will invest in achieving it.

A factor that helps you successfully incorporate values into your life is **wisdom.** Wisdom is not cleverness or knowledge or even intelligence. People rarely achieve a high position in government, business, or the workplace without intelligence and knowledge. But clever and intelligent people who end up in prison lack wisdom. Scandals at corporations involve highly intelligent, knowledgeable, and clever executives who appear to lack wisdom.

Intelligence without wisdom is a characteristic of those individuals who seek huge profits in making and distributing videos dealing with pornography and violence. Wisdom evaluates and sees them as degrading human dignity and desensitizing viewers to human suffering and pain.

Intelligent persons—especially professionals—can be difficult to influence. Their intelligence can block the understanding of their real needs and build a wall of denial and self-deception around the true cause of their troubles.

Wisdom is present when any entity—a government, an academic or a religious institution, a family, or a workplace—supports and respects the human spirit. This is demonstrated when an entity recognizes the innate rights, freedoms, and creativity of its members and makes every effort to help them realize their full potential. Helping individual members of an entity reach their potential supports it in reaching its fullest potential as well.

The more you are conscious of what is truly important in your life, the more you grow in wisdom. The more you face reality rather than escape into fantasy, the more you grow in wisdom.

The following list of values, adapted from Linda Kavelin-Popov's *The Virtues Project Educator's Guide,* will help you in setting your goals for personal growth:

assertiveness	diligence	integrity	reliability
caring	enthusiasm	joyfulness	respect
cleanliness	excellence	justice	responsibility
commitment	flexibility	kindness	self-discipline
compassion	forgiveness	love	service
confidence	friendliness	loyalty	tact
consideration	generosity	moderation	thankfulness
cooperation	gentleness	modesty	tolerance
courage	helpfulness	orderliness	trust
courtesy	honesty	patience	trustworthiness
creativity	honor	peacefulness	truthfulness
detachment	humility	perseverance	understanding
determination	idealism	purposefulness	unity

Being strong in these qualities will contribute to your success in all areas of your life. Take a moment and reflect on what that means to you. The word "success" has a different meaning for each of us.

For instance, Maya Angelou defines it as "liking yourself, liking what you do, and liking how you do it." Margaret Mead measures success "in terms of the contribution an individual makes to her or his fellow human beings." How do you define success?

10.2 RESPECTING YOURSELF

As you become more aware of your values and assess your present capabilities, attitudes, and behaviors, accepting yourself depends largely on how much you respect yourself. Three variables contribute to the degree to which you have this respect: **(1) self-esteem**, **(2) self-concept**, and **(3) self-confidence.**

Self-esteem is an inner view of how you feel about yourself. It affects your thinking and your actions, and it can either make or break you, depending on how positive or negative that self-esteem is. Consider the following illustration, taken from *Feeling Good* by John Burns:

> Almost all negative emotional reactions inflict their damage only as a result of low self-esteem. A poor self-image is the magnifying glass that can transform a trivial mistake into an overwhelming symbol of personal defeat. For example, Eric, a first-year law student, feels a sense of panic being in a class. "When the professor calls on me, I'll probably goof up."

Eric believes it would be terrible to be disapproved of, to make a mistake, or to fail. He seems convinced that if one person looked down on him, everyone would. It is as if the word REJECT was suddenly stamped on his forehead for everyone to see. He seems to have no sense of self-esteem that is not contingent on approval. He measures himself by the way others look at him. If his craving for approval and accomplishment are not satisfied, Eric senses that he would be nothing because there is no true support from within.

High self-esteem means strongly liking yourself. It means understanding who you are in the moment and accepting your feelings, thoughts, flaws, wants, needs, and desires. You believe you are entitled to your views and beliefs and are open to the possibility of change. You accept your limitations and strengths. This is what gives you the power to grow in your own esteem. There is only one person who can really control your self-esteem and that is you.

High self-concept means thinking highly about yourself. It means acknowledging your strengths, limits, and possibilities for growth and change in relationships at college and on the job. It's about waking up and being aware of yourself and how you relate to your environment. Hence, do not be afraid of what others think or say about you. After all, it is only their opinion. It does not need to be yours.

High self-confidence means you believe in yourself, that you have the competence and the motivation to accomplish a certain task or project. What appears to be risky to another, you see as challenging, and you believe you can do it. Self-confidence grows the more you take responsibility for yourself and the more your actions are successful.

Once you have a better grasp of who you are and how you behave through self-awareness and self-assessment, and once you are clear about your values and who you want to become based on those values, then it is a question of how much you respect yourself. To the degree that you like yourself, think highly of yourself, and have self-confidence, you can move forward to successfully achieve your goals of personal growth and development.

10.3 USING VISUALIZATION

One technique you will find valuable in your quest for personal growth is visualization. Visualization involves using your imagination to create what you want for yourself in your life. Louis Tice, author of *Visualization*, offers four easy steps in the visualization process:

1. Imagine clearly what exactly you would like to have happen in your life [your vision].
2. Affirm your vision over and over following the three P's:
   a. Personal: Use the first person pronoun "I." [I am free from smoking, and it feels wonderful.]
   b. Present: State your vision as though it were already happening. [I am getting A's in all my subjects. Wow! Am I happy!]
   c. Positive: Express your vision in terms of what you want, not what you do not want. [I am graduating from college and have taken a job with great potential.]
3. Picture yourself actually doing and living your vision and delighting in the feelings of success.
4. Picture your vision as you fall off to sleep at night, immediately upon awakening, and often during the day whenever your mind is in automatic mode—for example, when you're exercising.

Do these steps for at least a month to achieve progress toward your goals.

Here's the way a college student visualized achieving his goal:

> Wally was pursuing a degree in physical therapy. Every morning upon awakening and every evening while falling off to sleep, he closed his eyes and visualized himself as the physical therapist he wanted to become. He saw himself wearing a white lab coat. He visualized himself in the physical therapy department of Mount Pleasant Hospital, which had great facilities. The equipment shone in the morning sun. He saw himself checking his appointment book and preparing for the day's patients. He visualized that he would be seeing an elderly woman with osteoporosis, a child who broke his arm playing baseball, a career woman whose knee had been damaged in a fall, and a construction worker injured when a large barrel fell on his back.
>
> Wally heard himself speaking to each client, inquiring about symptoms and conditions. He saw himself gently responding to each client's physical disability with the appropriate exercises, encouraging each patient to try a little harder to meet his or her goal. He heard himself affirm their efforts and felt the satisfaction of being in a career where helping people was most important. He heard each patient thank him for helping them to improve. Coming out of his visualization, Wally felt encouraged and energized to continue studying. He realized that his career goal made his hard work worthwhile.

Actors, singers, musicians, artists, writers, speakers, and professional athletes also use visualization to improve their physical performance. Visualizing scenarios in their minds, they create all the specific details of the performances they want to achieve. With eyes closed, they carry out the perfect form needed for the successful activity. They enact the perfect performance repeatedly, until, after some time, the body connects with the mind in reproducing the perfect performance on command. The **mental archetype,** or perfect picture, becomes one with the physical act to create an improved performance.

Here's another example of visualization that you may find helpful:

> Rodney wanted to buy a special new car. He bought a piece of poster board and pasted color magazine photos of the car of his dreams on it. Then, surrounding the board, he printed the price he wanted to pay for the car and all the options he wanted. Every day Rodney spent ten minutes visualizing the car of his dreams. When he closed his eyes, he saw the color of the car, vivid and bright. He opened the driver's side door and slipped into the leather seat. He felt the comfort of the seat as he adjusted it. He turned the ignition key and listened to the purr of the motor. Then he took a deep breath, taking in that unmistakable new car smell.
>
> As the visualization became stronger each day, Rodney found it was easy to save the money he needed to purchase the car. In his visualizations, he used a collage of images that triggered the outcome he desired. He used all of his senses to become part of the experience of owning his own car. He visualized the final outcome. In the end, he found exactly the car he visualized and the money to pay for it.

Through models like Rodney's, you can customize your visualizations to your needs and goals. Remember it is a three-step process:

1. Say your affirmation over and over again using the first person pronoun "I." Be positive, state what you want, not what you don't want, and use the present tense. For example, "I am free from smoking."
2. Picture yourself doing what you say.
3. Feel yourself doing what you say. Enjoy those positive feelings.

10.4 SETTING GOALS

Setting goals is an important way to set priorities in your life, to guide your decisions, and to embody your values. At the same time, you need to be flexible enough to change your course if you learn new information and have new experiences. There are three types of goals you can pursue: (1) personal, (2) educational, and (3) career.

Personal Goals

Each of us has many areas of our lives and many wants and desires we would like to have fulfilled. Perhaps you'd like to learn French, or be a better uncle, or make more money. Perhaps you'd like to improve your math scores or become a better runner. Maybe your social life needs improvement, or you want to get married, or you want more time with your children. Having a personal mission means having fixed in your mind who you want to be at the end of a period.

High in the Sierra Nevada Mountains, reporters and well wishers gathered to congratulate Mark Wellman. In July 1989, Wellman and his friend Mike Corbett set out to scale El Capitan, one of the most challenging mountain summits in Yosemite National Park. Though it took them nine days, the pair achieved a dream they had spent seven years planning, ever since Wellman had become a paraplegic in a fall from another of Yosemite's peaks. In 90-degree heat and gusting winds, the climbers scaled El Capitan's 3200-foot cliff by moving six inches at a time! They succeeded because they prepared and carried out their plans inch by inch.

Educational Goals

From the time you enter elementary school, people start asking you what you want to be when you grow up. For most people, the answer changes numerous times as they are growing up. By the time you enter college, and certainly when you are partway through, you have a better idea of your talents and abilities and often some idea of what kind of career you want to have. Knowing what kind of job you want to find will obviously influence your choice of courses and your degree major.

As you start to clarify your career direction, you will find it helpful to start setting goals to get there. These might include taking aptitude tests, doing an internship, or setting up an informational interview with someone in a particular field. You might need to set a goal for the level of education you will need to achieve success in that career—do you need a master's degree? A Ph.D.? A medical degree? Once that goal is set, then you will need to set goals for obtaining the financing to pay for it! Remember, your college might have advisors, a career center, or other resources that can support you in your goals.

Selita is a first-year student at a community college. She wants to earn an associate's degree in respiratory therapy. Maryellen, her close friend, also attends the college, but she wants to earn a bachelor of science degree in nursing. Each day they drive to work with Andre, who wants to major in business. He plans to earn an associate's degree and a bachelor's degree, and then he plans to attend a high-quality graduate school where he can earn a master's degree in business administration. All three students have educational goals, although their goals are not the same.

Career Goals

It is no longer the case that a person is likely to stay in the same job all of his or her life. People often have many careers or positions over time. Part of what will determine if you should switch careers or jobs is whether the current position meets your career goals. You will need to have goals for your level of excellence in the job. How well do you want to be doing it; for example, how can you effectively meet your customer's needs? You will need to understand your personal growth and development needs—are you getting the ongoing training that you need? You will need to know how much money you want to make, what kind of relationship you want with your managers, in what kind of setting you want to work, how often you want to be promoted to positions of greater responsibility, what level at the company you want to achieve, and so on. Being clear about your career goals will help you to find a place where you can work happily—and help you determine when it is time to move on.

If you reach a point where you are unhappy in your position, then you will find it helpful to set goals for change. Do you want to go back to school? Do you need a mentor to help you make a transition to a new field? Do you need to do anything to better understand a new position before moving? Careful fact-finding and goal setting will help you make wise choices without regrets.

10.5 SETTING OBJECTIVES

An **objective** is a short-term action that helps you to attain your long-range goal. To accomplish your long-range goals, you need to be clear in identifying what is important to do each day to reach your goals. You can do this successfully by setting specific and concrete objectives for yourself.

Using the SMARTER System

Objectives are most successfully accomplished when they are structured according to the SMARTER system. SMARTER is an acronym formed by the following words:

- Specific
- Measurable
- Attainable
- Relevant
- Time-Phased
- Evaluated
- Rewarded

S: The Objective Needs to Be SPECIFIC The objective is **specific** when it is expressed in behavioral terms. The objective must be focused on something that a person *does*, rather that on what he or she *thinks* or *feels*. For example, Antonio knows that he has a negative attitude toward school assignments, and his first objective is to change this counterproductive attitude. This is not an objective Antonio is likely to achieve. His objective needs to be something specific that can be observed. Suppose instead he said something like this: "My objective is to sit down and study from 2:00 P.M. to 4:00 P.M. every day for the next week." That objective is behaviorally specific.

Take the example of Julie, who knows that she sometimes has a disrespectful attitude toward her supervisor, Ms. Chan. Suppose she says, "My objective is to change my attitude toward my supervisor." Again, this does not qualify as an objective. The objective needs to be some specific behavior that Julie engages in, such as, "Tomorrow, when I meet Ms. Chan, I am going to compliment her on the new program she is implementing."

M: The Objective Needs to Be MEASURABLE George wants to lose weight. He says to himself, "Every week, for the next eight weeks, I intend to lose a pound a week." That is a very good objective because it is measurable. At the end of one week, all George has to do is get on a scale to determine if he has indeed lost one pound during the previous seven days.

A cardiologist advises Alice to exercise more to reduce her high cholesterol level. Alice goes home and says, "My objective is to get more exercise." That's a good intention, but it does not qualify as an objective. Here's what Alice could have as an objective: "Every day for the next week I will walk a mile in twenty minutes." That's a behavioral objective that is also measurable. Every day Alice knows whether or not she has walked that mile in twenty minutes.

A: The Objective Needs to Be ATTAINABLE Objectives can cover a wide range—from being too easy to being challenging to being so difficult that it will be virtually impossible to attain them. If an objective is almost impossible to attain, you may see yourself as a failure when you don't meet it.

Kao Ping had a 2.3 grade point average (GPA) because he was struggling to improve his English along with learning the content of his courses. He wanted to set an objective to do better in the next semester. If he sets his objective at achieving a 4.0 GPA, he is likely to be disappointed and frustrated. Instead he sets an attainable goal of achieving a 2.9 GPA. The next semester he can then set an objective that is a bit higher.

R: The Objective Needs to Be RELEVANT The objective needs to be something relevant, or important, to you so you are motivated to attain it. A man may learn how to participate in road rallies to please his girlfriend, but if car trips are not important to him, the chances are he will not make a good navigator. A wife may take up golf to please her husband, but if her heart is not really into the game, she will find excuses not to play, and in time not play at all. If employees have relevant objectives and goals, they are more likely to succeed in the workplace. If Bob has the objective of being on the executive management team, then he will see the relevance of getting a master's degree in business administration.

T: The Objective Needs to Be TIME-PHASED Suppose Elena's educational goal is to earn an associate of arts degree at the local community college. She reads in the college catalog that she needs sixty semester hours of credit in the program she wants. Ordinarily, it will take a full-time student two years to complete the program. Elena, however, cannot become a full-time student because she needs to work full-time at her job. She will need to figure out how many credit courses she can fit in each semester. She needs to set a time-phased objective, such as the following: "Every semester for the next five years, I will take two courses at the community college." Elena could even make it more specific. She might say, "Since my goal is to earn an associate of arts degree in five years, my objective is to complete all the core courses in the first two years."

E: The Objective Needs to Be EVALUATED Did Elena achieve her objective? Did she accomplish all that she had intended? If her objective was truly a SMART objective, she will be able to evaluate it. She has graduated with an associate of arts degree and a 3.8 GPA. She views her success with great satisfaction. "I did well," she says to herself. She is proud of her accomplishments and so is her whole family.

R: The Objective Needs to Be REWARDED Having been successful in achieving a bachelor of arts degree, Elena decides to reward herself by taking a trip to New York City to enjoy three Broadway plays. The theater has always been an exciting experience for her, and never having been to New York, this reward will be an added thrill. The advantage in setting SMARTER objectives is that they help us to achieve those objectives and they enable us to see the bigger picture, which provides us with a range of alternatives.

■ TIPS FOR SUCCESS ■
Personal Growth

1. Practice self-awareness.
2. Listen carefully to feedback from others, and remember that most people give feedback not in a spirit of overt criticism but as helpful advice. You are always free to accept what you want or need and discard the rest.
3. Monitor your self-talk. Don't get down on yourself and call yourself names. Your best will change from day to day, depending on how you feel and your level of stress.
4. Look for your positive qualities. Continually emphasize what you do well, and tie that to other areas of your life that could be strengthened.
5. Be aware of the thoughts you have that disempower you, and substitute thoughts that open up possibilities for positive action.
6. Restate your thoughts and sentences so they are positive instead of negative.
7. Practice daily affirmations of your positive qualities and possibilities for growth, making certain your affirmations are positive, present tense, and personal.
8. Do a regular inventory of your progress in developing positive qualities.
9. Specifically visualize in your mind's eye successfully achieving each of your goals and objectives.

SCENARIO FOR SUCCESS

Analiese van Hahner has been in her position as a dietitian at United University Hospital for three months. She is approaching her first performance review, which is required to move beyond her new employee probationary period. She is nervous about the review, even though she believes her work has been satisfactory. When she meets with the manager, she is asked about her accomplishments, challenges, concerns, and self-assessment. She struggles to answer many of the questions. The weeks have been busy and challenging, and she isn't totally clear on her answers. The manager has observed her performance as satisfactory, however, so she is now a full-time employee.

Analiese is unwilling to go through a performance review unprepared again. She starts a performance folder and begins to make notes of specific accomplishments. When she receives praise or letters of appreciation from others, she makes a note of it or places a copy in her folder. When she develops a new procedure that improves the efficiency of her job, she makes a note for the folder. When it is time for her annual performance appraisal, Analiese reviews all of her notes and prepares a self-assessment report that includes details of her accomplishments. Her manager is able to more clearly acknowledge her contributions and reward her with an appropriate raise in salary.

Questions for Discussion

1. What do you think of Analiese's plan to prepare for her next performance review? Would it be possible for you to emulate any of her actions in college or work?
2. How have you handled what you perceived as negative feedback in the past?

3. What changes could you now make that would enable you to successfully profit from perceived negative feedback?
4. What could you do to proactively prepare for the performance appraisals in your life?

ACTIVITIES FOR SUCCESS

Activity 1: Visualizing Something Special

Visualization can empower you to create something new in your life that improves the quality of your experience.

Objectives: (1) To explore the possibilities of visualization; (2) to incorporate what you are learning to help achieve your goals.

Procedure:

Step 1: Sit down, relax, shut your eyes, and imagine yourself as a very successful person. This is your time to think of something special that you want to accomplish. Are you an inventor? Did you start your own business? Have you dedicated your life to the service of others? Are you a poet? A corporate lawyer? A full-time mother? A physician who has discovered a cure for HIV/AIDS? A corporate executive? A founder of an organization to help the poor, sick, or homeless? An accountant? A botanist? An accomplished musician? An inspired teacher? Here's a chance to visualize yourself as a success at whatever you would like to do with your life. Visualize yourself as that successful person.

Step 2: Write as many details in the present tense as you can think of to describe yourself as that successful person.

Step 3: Draw a picture to remind you of your visualization.

Step 4: Put yourself in the picture with what you want. Concentrate on this picture for three full minutes, and then place it near your bed or someplace where you are sure to see it every day. Each time you look at it, experience the wonderful feelings of having your vision happening for you. Keeping the vision alive will support you in developing specific goals and objectives that make the vision come true.

Activity 2: Growing in Self-Esteem

Improving self-esteem is a matter of choosing attitudes and actions that counteract negative beliefs and raise your sense of your own value.

Objective: To increase your growth in self-esteem.

Procedure: Choose and complete at least three of the following actions.

Step 1: Think of people you know who are positive about themselves. Notice how you feel about yourself when you are with them. Positive people look at life as an opportunity, not as an obligation. Notice how they use expressions, such as "I get to" and "I want to" rather than "I have to" or "I should." Notice, too, how they do not "should" all over others, but encourage others rather than give them advice. When you are successful, notice how they rejoice with you, rather than envy you.

Decide now to spend more time with people who esteem themselves. If possible, seek them out. When you are with these people, you may feel more free to be yourself, say what you think and feel, ask for what you need and want, and be willing to take risks.

Step 2: Make a list of things that you like to do. Give a copy to a friend or post the list on your mirror. Resolve to do one of these things each day for a week. Report in with a friend or check off items as you do them. Doing something for yourself sends a powerful message that no matter what else happens each day, you are nonetheless valuable and respect your own needs.

Step 3: Make a list of things that are uncomfortable for you to do, yet are activities you believe would bring you personal growth. The list might include things such as going by yourself to a film, a restaurant, or even on vacation. Perhaps it is doing something new that takes courage or skill such as kayaking, building something, or painting. Resolve to push your comfort zone outward by doing a different activity each day.

Step 4: Do something for someone else. You may wonder how this can help your self-esteem. It does, simply by letting you know that you are uniquely good and able to make a positive difference. When you make a contribution to someone, it can clarify your strengths and reinforce your positive self-esteem reflection.

Step 5: Each evening for a week, take a few minutes to look at your day. Record positive things that you can praise yourself for in each of the day's activities. You may notice "yes, but" creeping in to tell you the negative side of things. Ignore the negative and focus only on the positive.

Activity 3: Personal Growth

You block your ability to achieve success and growth when you do the following:

Deny your intuitive sense of the way things are.
React rather than respond.
Act out of self-pity instead of self-respect.
Be defensive rather than open.

Objectives: (1) To gain experience in self-honesty; (2) to replace "victim" thinking with "success" thinking.
Procedure: Group activity

Step 1: Rewrite the underlined sentences in the examples below to show that the person involved has improved his or her self-esteem and self-concept. Meet as a group to discuss your conclusions. Discuss what power each person gave away and how he or she could do things differently.

1. Deny your intuitive sense of the way things are:

   Juan is explaining to a friend his version of his relationship with his girlfriend, Julia: "Last Friday Julia didn't meet me at the mall. I waited for forty five minutes. Something probably came up preventing her from coming. The Friday before that she canceled our date because she wasn't feeling well. The previous Saturday her aunt and uncle were in town, and she couldn't get away, so we postponed our plans. But I know that she likes me and wants to be with me."

2. React rather than respond:

   Helene and Cheryl, two students living on campus, just finished having lunch together. "I can't find my wallet," Helene said to Cheryl.
   "I didn't take it, if that's what you're thinking," Cheryl snapped.
   "Did I say that?" Helen asked. "I thought if I told you about it, you might help me find it."

3. Act out of self-pity instead of self-respect:

   "What am I going to do?" Joe asked Ron. "Mr. Gonzalez won't give me an extension to turn in my research paper. He says that if the paper is not turned in on time, I will get docked a grade for every day it's late. He thinks that his course is the only one in the world."
   Ron answered, "He can't spring that on you. It isn't fair!"
   "Well, I have kind of known about it," Joe replied. "But I still don't think it's fair."
   "When did you find out about his policy?" Ron asked.
   "The first day of class," Joe answered as he bit his lower lip. "But still, I'm a busy person. I work, take three classes, and try to have a life. I think I'm going to complain to the division head."

4. Be defensive rather than open:

   Karen sat down with her supervisor to go over her job evaluation together. "Karen, I appreciate your punctuality and attendance," Mr. Ross said. "The quality of your work is excellent. You do your job very well. I'd like to suggest one way you could help to improve the quality of the department. Instead of working alone all the time, try to work as a team with the other employees. Working together produces more creative solutions to problems and contributes to a positive atmosphere."
   Karen crossed her arms and sat stiffly, frowning at Mr. Ross. "You said I do my job almost perfectly. I don't see what working with other people has to do with my evaluation," she said. "I work better alone. I like to control my own projects. Working with others takes more time and is often less productive. Besides, if you knew what goes on, Mr. Ross, you wouldn't be so quick to put me down," Karen replied.

JOURNAL FOR SUCCESS

Journal Entry 1

Clarity about your personal philosophy can guide many decisions and choices you make in your life.

Objectives: (1) To consider your personal philosophy on life; (2) to name the values you choose to live by; (3) to name the character traits that you acknowledge you already have or that you want to develop.

Procedure:

Step 1: Think about someone whose values you admire. Perhaps you want to consider people who are widely known for having the power of their convictions, like Abraham Lincoln, Gandhi, Mother Theresa, or the Reverend Martin Luther King, Jr. Perhaps you may want to consider a lesser-known hero, such as someone important in your life—a parent, sibling, or friend—someone who has remained true to his or her values and reflects that faithfulness in actions. When you have decided on a person, answer the questions below about him or her.

    1. What values are or were important to the person?

    2. How are these values demonstrated in the person's life? What actions show that the person lived for is living by these values? (For example, you may know a person who is physically challenged, perhaps someone who attends classes with you and is succeeding in the class. It appears that the person values education as well as the qualities of perseverance and self-respect.)

Step 2: Now turn inward to look at your own life and ask yourself these questions:

    1. What are the values you were taught early in your life?

    2. Where did they come from—your parents, school, religion, a friend, or the media?

    3. What values have you rejected?

    4. Do you know why they are no longer important to you?

    5. What happened that brought about these changes in what you deem important in your life? Notice how your values motivate you in making decisions and reflect on what you take for granted.

Step 3: Draft a personal philosophy statement. Here is an example:

Personal Philosophy of Rob Solenz

I am on this planet for a purpose. I want to make a difference in the lives of those who have no voice in our society. I am motivated by the values of fairness and mutuality. By this I mean that the earth and every living creature on our planet deserve respect and consideration, regardless of how society sees power. Each person is entitled to respect and fair treatment. I pledge to speak for those who have no voice in whatever ways I can.

Journal Entry 2

Imagine that you are reading you own obituary in the newspaper. You have had a long and healthy life. What accomplishments would you want to see listed? What would you want the obituary to say?

Objectives: (1) To project the accomplishment of a long-range goal; (2) to examine how you are targeting your goal in your daily decisions.

Procedure:

Step 1: Answer these questions:

    1. What three things do you want to keep on doing in your life now?

    2. What three things do you want to stop doing?

    3. What successes would you like to achieve by the end of your life?

Focusing on death may bother some of you, but it can help you get a feel for what goals you need and want to set in order to be successful.

Step 2: Write down your answers to the following questions: 1. What personal, educational, and career goals would you like to accomplish in your life? 2. Why is each goal important to you? 3. What do you need to do and what support do you need to accomplish your goals? 4. What objectives will help you to achieve your goals? Reflect on and choose at least one personal, one career, and one educational goal, then list the short-term objectives that will help you to attain your goals. Remember to use the SMARTER system in forming your objectives (Specific, Measurable, Attainable, Relevant, Time-Phased, Evaluated, and Rewarded).

CHAPTER 11
Developing Successful Communication Skills

Fully functioning persons are aware of the pitfalls of communication and therefore do not take it casually. They listen to the words they speak and those spoken to them.

—Leo Buscaglia

To Learn and Understand

- How can an understanding of one's own body language support personal growth?
- What are the steps to effective active listening?
- What are the steps to effective communicating?
- How do you communicate when you have a problem with someone?
- How do you communicate when someone has a problem with you?

11.1 BODY LANGUAGE

"What did you mean by *that*?" Carrie's mother asked.

"By *what*? I didn't say anything," Carrie replied.

"You didn't have to say anything," her mother said. "You gave me that *look*."

Nonverbal cues are the body movements and expressions that reveal a person's thoughts, emotions, and beliefs. According to Peter Dawson, author of *Fundamentals of Organizational Behavior,* some nonverbal cues "have a common meaning to most people of the same culture, and some have many meanings and require explanation by the user. If the communication is important, the exact meaning should be determined."

Some behaviors may be the result of nervous behavior or a way to act out boredom, but unless we clarify them the communication/message can be misinterpreted. As Dawson states, "Reading too much into a nonverbal cue may be worse than missing the cue completely." The most effective way to determine true meaning is to ask the sender to interpret his or her behavior.

Without proper communication, misunderstandings can and do happen all too often, resulting in anger, frustration, and fewer attempts at communication. We all have ways of communicating without saying a word. Our body language speaks for us. Carrie's mother recognized "the look" Carrie was giving her. Our body language provides various ways for us to communicate our feelings. Through our body language we may encourage or discourage intimacy, warn or invite, assert ourselves, or back down.

Table 11.1 indicates typical nonverbal behavior and how it is usually interpreted in American culture. The examples and their interpretations are not, by any means, definitive. The language of the body changes and varies from culture to culture, and some gestures may be either positive or negative, depending on the context in which they are used.

Cultural Differences

Body language and nonverbal communication differ widely in most cultures. There are few, if any, universal gestures. In *Intercultural Communication,* Leroy A. Samovar and Richard E. Porter suggest that some of the obvious differences revolve around touching, space, and eye contact.

Touching Touching is widely accepted as normal behavior in Latin America, in Arab and southern European cultures, and in some African cultures. In Western cultures, touching as an expression of affection is generally confined to the family, except for greetings and partings. It is common, for example, for a Brazilian manager to give a kiss to his female staff upon coming into the office and in leaving. For males, a friendly handshake with an

Table 11.1

Nonverbal Communication	Interpretation
Palm down (gesture when speaking)	Emphasis; self-confidence
Making a fist	Aggressiveness; positive reinforcement; congratulations
Leaning in toward the other	Interest; active listening; intimidation
Crossing the arms	Self-protection; defensive stance; perhaps disagreement
Scratching the head	Perplexity
Raising eyebrows	Surprise; disagreement
Lowering eyebrows	Puzzlement; anger
Pursed lips	Tenseness; critical attitude
Standing too close to another	Disrespect for someone's personal space; intimidation (varies according to culture)
Blank facial expression	Disrespect; lack of interest
Nodding the head vertically	Active listening; understanding; agreement (varies with culture)
Nodding the head horizontally	Disagreement
Repeated tapping on a surface	Nervousness; impatience; thinking
Looking at one's watch or clock	Impatience; time concern
Meeting another's gaze	Interest; respect (varies according to culture)
Not meeting another's gaze	Shame; deceit; fear; lack of interest (varies according to culture)
Laughter/smile	Enjoyment; nervousness; submission
Hand on chin	Thinking
Swaggering walk	Dominance; strength; pride; arrogance
Clearing the throat	Nervousness; time filler; attention-seeking
Fingering of tie, earrings, etc.	Nervousness; fear; boredom
Wringing of hands	Tension; indecision; fear
Folding hands	Receptivity to the speaker; calmness

affectionate touch on the shoulder is common. In North America, where such communication would be considered suspect, and therefore avoided, appreciation and respect are expressed mostly through words.

Space   Latin Americans, Arabs, and southern Europeans prefer being very close when communicating and interpret distance in space as indicating distance in a particular relationship. North Americans and northern Europeans stand much farther apart from one another, and they view closeness as a message of amorous intention or a threat of attack. An elaborate set of rules in the caste system of India has traditionally prescribed exactly how close people can come to each other.

Eye Contact   For Arabs and Latin Americans, eye contact is important, and often trustworthiness is communicated by a willingness to look the other in the eyes while communicating. Lack of eye contact in these cultures is generally interpreted as being impolite, dishonest, or disinterested. For northern Europeans and North Americans, however, eye contact with strangers is generally not practiced except when endeavoring to make a sale or obtain a favor. Among friends and colleagues, eye contact is expected and appreciated. Asians, particularly, interpret eye contact on the part of individuals of lower social status as disrespectful, insulting, and even threatening.

Other Cultural Differences   Some cultures are far more demonstrative than others, such as the Italians compared to the British. To understand an Italian, you need to pay attention to what the hands are saying as well as the words.

Greetings are expressed in many different ways as well. Westerners shake hands. People from Japan and Thailand tend to bow, and the greater the status of the other, the deeper the bow. Indians may place hands together, saying "Namaste," which means "I honor the place in you where the entire universe resides; I honor the place in you of love, of light, of truth, of peace. . . ."

Tone of voice varies in different cultures. Arabs tend to speak loudly. North Americans speak louder than Europeans, which is sometimes interpreted as assertiveness or even arrogance, giving Americans a somewhat negative reputation in other countries.

Saving face and maintaining harmony, even at the expense of being honest from the Westerner's point of view, is common among Asians. A head nod, for example, rarely means agreement, but simply understanding. "Yes" can mean "yes," but it can also mean "If you say so" or "I hope I have said this unenthusiastically enough for you to understand that I mean 'no.'"

Hence, paying attention to body language, tone of voice, and other nonverbal communication is particularly important when you are interacting with people from different cultures. A good start is to develop an open mind toward the practices of other cultures. Rather than believing that the way you communicate is the right and proper way, enjoy and learn from the differences in others.

11.2 ACTIVE LISTENING

Michael and Gail were attending the wedding of friends. At the reception, they sat with Mia and John, a couple they did not know, but who were also friends of the newlyweds. To make conversation, Michael asked Mia what high school she had attended. Mia said, "I went to Westport High. I got a good education, but it wasn't easy to be in the same school with my mother. She taught Earth Science." Michael, distracted by the newlyweds cutting the cake, heard only the "Westport High" part of Mia's response. He said to her, "I went to Westport High for two years. Then I had this terrible Earth Science teacher who ruined my attitude toward school and caused me to drop out." Mia got up from the table and walked away. "I will not allow anyone to speak that way about my mother," she called to Michael as she left the table. Michael turned to Gail. "How was I supposed to know that the Earth Science teacher was her mother?" Michael complained. "She told you," Gail replied. "You weren't listening."

One of the effects of not listening, as most of us have learned from experience, is missing something important. Sometimes we get by with **selective listening**, where we hear only what we want to hear. We are all too familiar with doing several things at once, such as watching television, reading, talking with others, and doing household chores.

Significantly, active listening, which necessitates paying attention, is not universally encouraged in our society where time is at a premium, and chats with neighbors are more the exception than the rule. Yet active listening is an important skill necessary for relating well with people, being successful at school or on the job, and even for being promoted. Whether we are talking with family, friends, work associates, school associates, or in whatever situation we find ourselves, active listening creates the possibility for better relationships. It creates a connection between people, and it empowers both the listener and the speaker.

Characteristics of Active Listeners

Active listeners usually exhibit the following characteristics:

1. *They listen carefully without interrupting inappropriately.* Because of perceived time pressures and perhaps impatience, you may sometimes want to interrupt someone who is speaking to you or finish his or her sentences. You may think you know better or can anticipate what the speaker will say. Rather than interrupting, it is better to give the speaker the freedom to describe the situation as it appears to him or her, carefully listening without interrupting.

2. *They acknowledge what is being said with appropriate eye contact and body language.* To communicate undivided attention to and understanding of what the speaker is saying, use verbal and nonverbal cues, such as the nod of the head or a simple "yes." Good eye contact without staring is essential for communicating interest. If you look down, gaze out the window, write, watch TV, play on the computer, or talk to someone else on the telephone, you are communicating that the speaker's time and words are not important to you. Active listening enables you to demonstrate the level of respect you have for another person.

3. *They ask questions for clarity.* At appropriate times, the active listener asks questions for clarity. However, be careful to avoid using questions to lead the speaker to your particular solution or outcome, just as a lawyer often does in attempting to lead a witness in court. Such behavior suggests that you believe you have all the answers. This develops dependency in the speaker and can cause the person to stop thinking independently. Instead, as the listener, ask open-ended questions such as, "What happened then?" "How did you feel?" "What do you think you can do now?" Notice how such questions require more than a "yes" or "no" response. Unlike advice, such questions promote greater understanding both for the speaker and the listener.

4. *They paraphrase.* By accurately **paraphrasing**—expressing another person's ideas in your own words—an active listener reinforces the speaker's statements, setting up an environment where there is a mutual understanding between the listener and the speaker. Paraphrasing helps you to understand what the speaker is saying and to some extent how the speaker feels. For example: "What I hear you saying is that you are not ready to openly discuss the problem with her" or "Let me see if I understand what you are saying. You are feeling upset about how your manager responded to your dilemma." By using this kind of phrasing, the listener assumes the responsibility for any failure in understanding and can attempt to rectify it. If the paraphrase is accurate, the speaker has the satisfaction of knowing that the point has been clearly understood.

5. *They empathize.* Empathy is not the same as sympathy. **Sympathy** is a compassionate expression of pity or sorrow for the misfortune of another; **empathy** is the ability to really understand and be sensitive to another person's feelings. It places the listener in the speaker's shoes, helps him or her walk a mile in another's moccasins, as Native Americans say. When you are empathetic, you perceive and evaluate an issue from another person's point of view. You endeavor to experience what he or she is experiencing. Empathy is often demonstrated nonverbally by a sensitive expression on your face, an understanding tone of voice, reaching out to touch the person's hand, or using other body language appropriate to one's culture (see Section 11.1).

11.3 SUCCESSFUL COMMUNICATION BEHAVIORS

High-tech communication systems surprise us daily with new and more efficient ways of transferring information between machines, computers, people, companies, and countries. We are in the middle of an information superhighway, and there is no stopping the innovations yet to come. In our personal relations, however, communication can easily bog down and even close down. Our human communication dynamic is still a hit-or-miss proposition, sometimes effective, yet at other times blocked by misunderstandings and **projections**—the perceptions and feelings within ourselves that we place on the person with whom we are communicating. For instance, someone who is feeling angry may perceive that someone else is hostile. Another classic example of projection occurs when a mother shivers from a cold draft and immediately puts a coat on her child.

Five communication behaviors can help you to communicate effectively. Together they are sometimes referred to as **leveling** with another:

1. *Be direct.* Speaking directly to the person with whom you have a concern makes sense, yet many people prefer to tell a number of coworkers or friends about a difficulty or disappointment, and say nothing to the person who can do something about it. This is called **triangulating**—a process in which three parties are involved in a communication but not directly with each other. The reason for triangulating may be the person's preference to be a passive victim, wanting attention and possibly sympathy. Speaking directly to the person with whom we have a problem is generally the adult thing to do, even if we are afraid or inexperienced. (*Note:* An exception to this is when you are in a dangerous or abusive situation, and you turn to a third party or an authority for assistance.)

   People who are responsible about communicating directly become aware of the powerful impact of their words. With each direct exchange, they experience less fear and more power. It's true that we can all find excuses for not speaking directly. We say, "The other person will hold it against me" or "I may put my job in jeopardy" or "The instructor may fail me if I speak up." There is no guarantee that these events will not occur; however, most of the time, people are reasonable if you choose your tone, language, and content with the intent to help and not to hurt anyone. Even if they do not agree with you, they usually respect and appreciate your willingness to bring up a concern with them. By talking it over directly, you may be helping the other person to see things differently.

   In addition, triangulating often causes problems to grow larger and disunity to increase. Backbiting and gossip have a negative effect on all parties, and they can be highly destructive to the productivity of a classroom or workplace. If you need to devise strategies for dealing with a problem, you can journal, or find a neutral, confidential party to work with you on brainstorming solutions. Once you have worked through clarifying the issues, however, the key to resolution is to communicate directly.

2. *Be accurate and complete.* For successful communication to take place, the participants need to transmit accurate messages. This means telling everything relating to the issues, not just the parts that make them look good. Selective "truth-tellers" may assign blame to others or they may rationalize their situation rather than take responsibility for their own actions. When you send a message that distorts your reality, you deny the power within you that comes from the accurate representation of your message. Fudging the truth—adjusting the accurate representation of the event—may be a short-term resolution to an immediate issue, but in the long run it short-circuits your success. For example, if you hate your job but tell others and yourself it's okay, you weaken yourself and will likely never tap the power necessary to motivate yourself to look for a job that you would enjoy and be successful at doing. In addition, people count on information to make decisions and take actions. If they receive only part of the information, their actions are often ineffective, even damaging.

3. *Be honest.* Honest communication includes what we do not say, as well as what we do say. Honesty demands that we acknowledge what we perceive, "rocking the boat" and disrupting things if necessary. When we maintain the status quo without speaking up, it is like ignoring the presence of an elephant in the living room. Everyone knows it is there, but no one wants to talk about it, so they pretend it does not exist. Lying damages trust in your relationships. People learn not to count on what you say, whether it is true or not.

4. *Be open.* Open communication allows for exchanges between authentic people who express their wants and needs. The strong survivor types who act like they need no one risk having poor relationships. They cut themselves off from others in the belief that if they reveal their feelings, they will be laughed at or disregarded. At the same time you need to respect your **boundaries**—how close you can wisely let someone be to you—and your need for confidentiality when you consider revealing part of your life to others. A bad experience in the past, however, does not mean that everyone is against you. When you have the strength to be open, others see you as approachable. The communication strengthens your inner power.

   Another barrier to open communication is **people-pleasing**. People who agree with everyone about everything choose to give up their own identities in order to gain acceptance from others. The irony of people-pleasing is that usually people are not pleased with the people-pleaser. Most people see through the shallow acquiescence of those who fear being themselves. Open communication reveals the inner power and beauty of you as a person. Others then can be comfortable and open with you in turn, producing greater intimacy. This is particularly applicable to Western culture. In many Eastern cultures, especially in Asia, harmony is valued more than openness, which can lead to being "nice" even when one does not feel in harmony with another person's ideas.

5. *Be timely.* It is important to take care of issues that bother you as they arise, even at the risk of some discomfort. If you don't, you may end up holding onto grudges and resentments that block you from participating in new personal growth that is natural in life. When you are closed up about a concern, you risk adding another load of baggage to your already overloaded shoulders. Some people carry past slights or injuries for years, savoring the memory of their victimization and enhancing their specialness, as they see it. As a result, they become disgruntled and depressed and often project these feelings onto other situations. Acknowledging errors and making amends free individuals from pain, open lines of communication, and maintain relationships. Timely communication enables people to take action to resolve an issue before it becomes a major problem.

Communicating Feelings

Personal communication involves risk-taking because it often includes the communication of feelings. Clinical psychologist Marshall B. Rosenberg, author of *Nonviolent Communication: A Language of Compassion,* has developed a four-point personal communication system that acknowledges the complexity of effective interpersonal communication. He calls it "giraffe" language, since it involves "sticking your neck out" to express your feelings through "I" statements.

It can be used when you wish to express positive feelings, or when you have a problem with another's behavior. Rosenberg identifies the four elements of his communication system:

   The first element is "When I (see, hear) _____"

   The second element is "I feel _____"

The third element is "because I am (needing) _____"
The fourth element is "and I would like you to _____"

Let's see how this works. The speaker acknowledges his or her feelings by using the four elements above. Here are three statements that might be based on these:

1. "I felt frustrated when you came home late because I was hoping we'd be able to get some front-row seats."
2. "When you said you'd do it and then didn't, I felt disappointed because I wanted to be able to rely upon your words."
3. "I'm irritated when you leave company documents on the conference room floor, because I want our documents to be safely stored and accessible."

By naming the internal association that causes the emotion, the speaker is communicating on a personal level and opening up the possibility for a personal exchange with the other person. The speaker is also taking responsibility for his or her own feelings and not **labeling** the other person in a negative or critical way because of his or her behavior. Labeling might sound like this:

- You're inconsiderate.
- You're always neglecting me.
- You're stupid.

Labeling usually causes the listener to become defensive and/or angry, which causes positive and mutual communication to stop.

Rosenberg suggests using another four-step process when you wish to respond empathically to another person who is upset with you.

1. "When you see me do _____"
2. "Do you feel _____"
3. "Because you are (needing) _____"
4. "And would like me to _____"

Again, let's see how this works. Person B makes an effort to understand what Person A is feeling and needing. Here are two examples:

1. "Person A: 'I've been a nervous wreck planning for my daughter's wedding. Her fiancé's family is not helping. About every day they change their minds about the kind of wedding they would like.'
   Person B: 'So you're feeling nervous about how to make arrangements and would appreciate it if your future in-laws could be more aware of the complications their indecision creates for you?'"
2. "Person A: 'You aren't God!'
   Person B: 'Are you feeling frustrated because you would like me to admit that there can be other ways of interpreting this matter?'"

If you make statements like this, you are empathically placing yourself in the other person's shoes and trying to guess both how the individual is feeling and what that person wants you to do. Even when you experience blame or criticism, you respond with care and empathy. Rosenberg calls this nonviolent communication, since it has a disarming effect on both parties.

11.4 PUBLIC SPEAKING AND MAKING PRESENTATIONS

Surveys show that the biggest fear people have is public speaking (although most people can make great speeches to themselves in the mirror!). Your heart rate might speed up, your hands get sweaty, and your mind goes blank. You become convinced that the audience is going to be hostile or not accept what you say. Shifting that outlook is half the battle in making a presentation. And, since public speaking and making presentations successfully are critical skills for success in college and in the workplace, it pays to come up with strategies for doing them well.

One of the most famous organizations for helping people become polished speakers is Toastmasters International. The following pointers from that organization have helped thousands of people become excellent speakers:

Tips For Successful Public Speaking*

Feeling some nervousness before giving a speech is natural and healthy. It shows you care about doing well. But, too much nervousness can be detrimental. Here's how you can control your nervousness and make effective, memorable presentations:

1. Know the room. Be familiar with the place in which you will speak. Arrive early, walk around the speaking area, and practice using the microphone and any visual aids.
2. Know the audience. Greet some of the audience as they arrive. It's easier to speak to a group of friends than to a group of strangers.
3. Know your material. If you're not familiar with your material or are uncomfortable with it, your nervousness will increase. Practice your speech and revise it if necessary.
4. Relax. Ease tension by doing exercises.
5. Visualize yourself giving your speech. Imagine yourself speaking, your voice loud, clear, and assured. When you visualize yourself as successful, you will be successful.
6. Realize that people want you to succeed. Audiences want you to be interesting, stimulating, informative, and entertaining. They don't want you to fail.
7. Don't apologize. If you mention your nervousness or apologize for any problems you think you have with your speech, you may be calling the audience's attention to something they hadn't noticed. Keep silent.
8. Concentrate on the message—not the medium. Focus your attention away from your own anxieties, and outwardly toward your message and your audience. Your nervousness will dissipate.
9. Turn nervousness into positive energy. Harness your nervous energy and transform it into vitality and enthusiasm.
10. Gain experience. Experience builds confidence, which is the key to effective speaking.

■ TIPS FOR SUCCESS ■
Communications

1. Be aware of your body and your movements and how they affect others.
2. Study other cultures to become aware of differences in the way people from various cultures communicate.
3. Be aware of the feelings you have that may affect how a message is being communicated.
4. Actively listen to others to experience more fully both who they are and how you really feel about them and what they are saying.
5. Recognize negative surprises and respond promptly and with empathy.
6. Use the five communication behaviors to help you communicate effectively.
7. Use Rosenberg's nonviolent communication methodology.
8. Take advantage of opportunities to practice public speaking.

SCENARIO FOR SUCCESS

Pete Halifan is 6 feet 5 inches tall with the build of a football player. He approaches people confrontationally and uses his body to intimidate others. His face often looks fierce and frowning. He is a team leader for five employees responsible for developing a marketing strategy for a new line of juices for Fizz International Bottling Company. The first team meeting is a disaster. No one communicates their ideas because they perceive that Pete is dominating the meeting. His manager has a coaching session with him, and Pete calls another meeting. This time he stays seated instead of standing over everyone. He starts to recognize that these employees are part of his team, not opponents. He is conscious of his facial expressions and deliberately smiles more. He poses open-ended questions and waits for others to contribute to the brainstorming instead of dictating ideas to others. This time the meeting results in a draft proposal.

*Copyright 1998 Toastmasters International (**www.toastmasters.com**).

Questions for Discussion

1. Does Pete Halifan exhibit any behavior you might imitate to be an effective communicator?
2. How might communication in the meeting change if the team members are from different cultures?
3. What tips for success have you utilized in the past to communicate successfully?
4. What communication techniques do you see yourself using in the future to communicate even more successfully?

ACTIVITIES FOR SUCCESS

Activity 1: Empowering Others Through Active Listening

The following experiment puts you in the role of a speaker, a listener, an advice giver, and an observer. Take note of what it is like for you to be in each position so that you can share your experience in the debriefing portion of the experiment.

Objectives: (1) To experience the benefits of listening rather than giving or getting advice; (2) to experience and share how it feels to be speaker, listener, advice giver, and observer.

Procedure: Work in groups of four participants.

Step 1: Agree among the four participants who will take the following roles.

- *Speaker:* Thinks of and then presents to the listeners a small dilemma; takes a minute to explain the dilemma.
- *Listener:* Actively listens to the speaker while asking questions in order to clearly understand the issue; does *not* tell the speaker what to do to solve the dilemma.
- *Advice giver:* Listens to the speaker and tells him or her exactly how to handle the dilemma; tells the speaker dogmatically what he or she would do in the same situation.
- *Observer:* Takes notes on observations, including both verbal and nonverbal cues; should focus especially on the effectiveness of active listening versus giving advice.

Processing/Debriefing

1. Speaker shares with the others what it was like to experience active listening versus getting advice. Indicate what role was most helpful in deciding what to do to solve the dilemma.
2. Listener shares what it was like to listen carefully and ask significant questions to better understand the speaker's dilemma.
3. Advice giver shares with others what it was like to tell the speaker how to solve the dilemma.
4. Observer shares what cues he or she observed, both verbal and nonverbal, focusing especially on the effectiveness of asking questions versus giving advice.

Activity 2: Body Language

Awareness of your own body language and that of others empowers you. Recognizing your own facial expressions and those of others, as well as body postures and the need for personal space, enables you to communicate your inner power and to acknowledge the messages of others.

Objectives: (1) To recognize body language signals; (2) to become sensitive to your own comfort zones and those of others.

Procedure: Work in small groups.

Step 1: This activity explores what is already known about body language. Each student picks a number from 1 to 10. The numbers correspond to postures from the list below. Each student portrays a body posture, and the other members of the group "read" its meaning, stating their interpretations of the behavior.

1. blank facial expression
2. slouched posture
3. whistling
4. foot tapping

5. clapping hands
6. leaning forward
7. head buried in hands
8. crossed arms
9. raised eyebrows
10. yawning and looking at one's watch

Step 2: Compare your group's answers with those of other groups. What answers came through fairly consistently? What postures had various interpretations? What did you learn about body language?

Step 3: Body language and its meaning differ from culture to culture. In one culture or region it is respectful to look at a person directly when speaking, while in another culture looking directly at the speaker is considered offensive. Research and share with the class your understanding of particular body language messages from a different culture or region. Explain how the body language differs in culture and in effect.

Step 4: We all have invisible fences around us to keep people at a certain distance. The diameter of the fence varies from culture to culture and from person to person. If you are in a person's space as you attempt to communicate, what you are saying will not be completely heard. Each of us needs a certain amount of space to feel comfortable.

The only time others are entitled to cross our invisible fences is when we invite them to do so. This invitation may be by gesture or words. In pairs, experiment with spatial relationship. First, stand so that you create too much distance between yourself and your partner. Then stand too close to each other. Finally, stand at a distance from each other that respects each person's boundaries, but is not unfriendly. Ask another student to draw the imaginary boundary circles of you and your partner in chalk on the floor. Share your "measurements" with the class and discuss your findings.

Activity 3: Personal Communication

It is important for the quality of relationships for people to be able to communicate their feelings effectively.

Objectives: (1) To become familiar with how to express "I" statements; (2) to appreciate that "I" statements do not blame or shame.

Procedure:

Step 1: Read and discuss Marshall Rosenberg's interpretation of the following example:

"SPEAKER: 'I feel happy that you received that award.'

ROSENBERG: To express the needs and thoughts underlying his or her feelings, the speaker might have said, 'When you received that award, I felt happy because I was hoping you'd be recognized for all the work you'd put into the project.' "

This statement is an example of "giraffe talk"—a formula that involves revealing your feelings to another person. Here are some other examples:

1. "I feel angry when you say that, because I am wanting respect and I hear your words as an insult."
2. "I'm discouraged because I would have liked to have progressed further in my work by now."
3. "I am grateful that you offered me a ride because I was needing to get home before my children."

Step 2: In small groups, create five examples modeled after Rosenberg's. Share your examples with the class.

Activity 4: Communication Behaviors

Observation is an important element in effective communication at all levels. By paying attention to what is happening, a person can provide accuracy in communicating events.

Objectives: (1) To accurately represent information; (2) to recognize when and how information is presented in an incomplete or inaccurate way.

Procedure: Work as a whole class.

Step 1: As an experiment to test the power of observation in the transmission of facts, your teacher will give three of your classmates the same page or paper to read, perhaps a recent page of a newspaper or magazine. Separately, your classmates will each scan the page for one minute and then write down from memory what they remember seeing.

Step 2: After they have written down their observations, they then share them with the class. Discuss the following as a class:
   1. How were their observations similar? Different?
   2. What conclusions can you draw about how people take in and transmit "facts"?
   3. What suggestions can you offer to make the transmission of information more accurate?

JOURNAL FOR SUCCESS

Journal Entry

   Objective: To become more aware of how you communicate with others to get your needs met and to respond to the needs of others.

   Procedure: After doing one of the activities above, write a journal entry describing what was of value for you and predict how this change in behavior may enable you to be more successful in the future.

CHAPTER 12
Building Teams Successfully

What makes us human is the way in which we interact with other persons. We learn how to interact within groups, through which we become socialized and educated.

—David W. Johnson and Roger T. Johnson

To Learn and Understand

- What is cooperation? What is collaboration?
- What is consultative decision making?
- What are some qualities of an effective team player?
- How can team members manage conflict?

12.1 COOPERATION AND COLLABORATION

An English composition class does peer review of writing assignments. A medical team at Metro Hospital successfully completes a heart transplant. A college academic team wins a contest. The Ishano family holds an annual reunion. Four musicians stage a jazz marathon to benefit AIDS patients. A student group creates a new invention.

The success of the above teams is directly linked to their ability to **cooperate** with each other. This means working peacefully, without serious conflict, and actively looking for ways to assist each other and the team in being successful. They must also **collaborate** with each other, which in this context means drawing on each others' ideas, skills, and talents, fully utilizing the best each individual can give for the outcome that is best for the team.

In college and in the workplace, teams are becoming increasingly common. Shared decision making is the new model for most offices—authoritarian dictates are moving toward being a thing of the past. When a team effectively **consults** together, commitment and trust are the outcome. This in turn results in a team that is highly productive and much-valued. Consultation requires that all team members participate with full and honest input into all discussions. It requires full fact finding, openness with no secrets, and team commitment to all decisions. The steps for consultative decision making are presented later in this chapter.

Working together is engaging, challenging, and rewarding. When a team is created for a common purpose, each member brings strengths and talents to the group. The resulting **synergy**—the combined energy of a group—creates opportunities for interacting with others and achieving results that could not be accomplished by one person alone. As you work cooperatively as a team member, you will come to learn who you are, what you stand for, and what you want and need in your interactions with others.

In every field of endeavor, leaders know they cannot achieve success alone. They want and need team players. Leaders know that teamwork is what will set their organizations apart in the twenty-first century. The rugged and often rigid individualist is finding less and less acceptance in society.

The Cooperative Tradition

Native Americans have a tradition of cooperation that has existed for thousands of years. In *Wisdomkeepers* by Steve Wall and Harvey Arden, a spokesperson for the Six Nations Iroquois Confederacy, explains the cooperative decision-making process used by the confederacy:

> We are made up of Six Nations. Each of us is equal. Each of us is sovereign. And we come together in a Confederacy. Our business is peace, not war. . . . In issues of peace and war and other major matters we sit together and make our decisions. There is no single author-ity. We do not vote. We must reach a decision that everyone agrees with. . . . A problem is presented from what we call the Well. From there it goes to each of the sides for discussion. Each side agrees or disagrees among itself and sends its decision on the problem back to the Well. There it is adjusted to conform with the decisions of the others. Then it's sent back out from the Well again. This goes on until the issue is unanimously decided. This is a very old Indian-style government. It requires complete unity of decision. It takes time. But the decisions, once made, are very firm. If there's a problem we can't seem to resolve, we re-consider it another time. If, after a third time, there's still no unanimous decision, then the Tadodaho, or presiding chief—who comes from the Onondaga, the keepers of the Central Fire—will announce a compromise decision. But if the problem is still divisive, the Tadodaho will say, "We will not address it at all, because there's no problem that's important enough to cause divisions among the people. The Peacemaker, who founded our Confederacy told us, we must be of one mind. Those are good words to remember today— or any day.

This configuration of cooperative decision making may seem idealistic in our fast-paced world. However, organizations are adapting the principles of team building and group decision making to fit our society's needs. They realize that the person who knows how to work with groups, solve problems with groups, and manage diversity in groups will be an asset to the academic world, business, industry, human services systems, and gov-ernment. People who learn to cooperate and collaborate broaden their awareness and knowledge by interacting with people having different viewpoints. They also have an opportunity to experience a range of leadership roles and heighten their self-esteem and sense of belonging in the process. People who work with others often enjoy their work more than people who work alone.

12.2 EFFECTIVE GROUP DECISION MAKING

You will be required throughout your academic and work life to make decisions regularly. At times, you will eas-ily make them by yourself, but often the decisions are more effective if you involve other people. It takes practice and skill to make decisions that are the best possible ones. It takes even more skill and practice to make them as a team. It's a skill worth learning, however. If you pool ideas and build on each others' contributions, you can often find creative solutions you never would have come up with on your own.

Consultative Decision-Making Steps

The following sequence of steps can facilitate the process of reaching effective decisions, a process sometimes referred to as consultative decision making:

1. *Focus:* It is wise to start with a period of calm focusing. In a business setting, the group leader might remind the team of the mission of the company. In a college project, the team leader might remind everyone of the goal. In a setting where people are comfortable with inspiration or prayer, a reading or prayer might start the group session.

2. *Gather the facts:* An effective decision must have accurate information at its foundation, not conjecture. This may require research, or it may simply require some discussion and gathering of data that people in the group already know. If there are background materials that relate to the topic, they are helpful to have at the meeting for reference.

3. *Agree on the issue:* Often a group will start out believing it knows what the issue is that requires a decision. However, once research and information gathering have been done, the perspectives of group members may change. Agreeing on the issue will prevent the group from trying to come up with actions that do not really address the issue.

4. *Understand the root cause:* This is an integral part of agreeing on the issue and devising solutions and actions. It is a process of asking questions about the issue: Why is this going on? How did it happen? What caused this? These questions and many more will help the group to maintain its focus on the right issue.

5. *Agree on principles that apply to the issue:* This is a key step that groups often miss. There are often foundation principles in the ethics or mission statements of a company, the code of conduct of a college, the belief system of an organization, or in the personal beliefs of the individuals involved that need to be identified to make an effective decision. These might include the insistence that justice happens, that truth is told even if it is difficult to do so, that people are treated with respect, that the environment is protected, that going into debt is to be avoided, and so on.

6. *Full and frank discussion:* Everyone's voice and perspective contributes to the discussion of the issue at hand and possible conclusions. When discussing alternative actions, it is often beneficial to try **brainstorming**—a process of quickly writing down all possible ideas without evaluation, which allows ideas to spark off each other. At the end of this process the group can then pick the ideas it thinks might work using whatever criteria make sense or are feasible. If lack of time or money are limiting factors, for example, staying within a certain budget or finding an intervention that can be completed before the end of the year would be relevant criteria.

7. *Pause for review:* It is a good idea for the chairperson/facilitator to check in with everyone to make sure everything pertinent has been said and that everyone is comfortable with the direction in which the group is going.

8. *Reach a decision:* Everyone may be ready to move toward a firm decision, or it may be obvious that the group has already reached a **consensus,** that point at which the majority of group members support a decision. Some groups will take a vote at this stage by a show of hands or doing a quick paper balloting. In other circumstances, someone will make a motion that a particular action be taken, and there will be a vote on the motion. Whatever process is followed, it is wise for the group leader to state the decision so it is clear to each member of the group what he or she is agreeing to.

9. *Plan for implementation and follow-up:* Once a decision has been made, the group needs to move into planning. The action steps for implementing the decision, also called objectives, must be clearly outlined with target completion dates. A system needs to then be put in place so that progress can be tracked. This will likely include additional group meetings.

10. *Evaluation:* It is wise to pause at various stages of the implementation process to evaluate the effectiveness of the actions underway. At the end of the process, the group will also need to assess whether the solution really did address the original issue effectively.

Creating Synergy

When individuals work on their own, the result is less than it would be if the work were done by a team. When a team works in synergy, the whole is greater that the sum of the parts because the team members build upon each others' ideas and encourage and support each other. This often brings about 15 to 20 percent greater

productivity, which means that more results are produced. Hence, it is in the interests of all to collaborate with others as they strive for success in college and at work.

Synergy in classrooms might include a team that forms to work on a science experiment and discovers a new way of accomplishing it. Synergy in the workplace might occur when a team meets to discuss low employee morale and creates a new method to positively influence the motivation of employees.

Teams may find it helpful to follow a set of principles for group consultation or synergy that have been effective in some organizations and companies. The following ten principles were designed by Idea Connection Systems:

Ten Principles for Creating Synergy

Note: The practice of these principles, like any art form, takes time. These principles are effective—not immediately efficient.

1. Respect each participant and appreciate each one's diversity. This is the prime requisite for consultation.
2. Value and consider all contributions. Belittle none. Withhold evaluation until sufficient information has been gathered.
3. Contribute and express opinions with complete freedom.
4. Carefully consider the views of others; if a point of view has been offered, accept it as your own as well.
5. Keep to the mission at hand. Extraneous conversation may be important to team-building, but it is not consultation. Consultation is solution driven.
6. Share in the group's unified purpose—desire for success of the mission.
7. Expect the truth to emerge from the clash of differing opinions. Optimum solutions emerge from a diversity of opinion.
8. Once stated, let go of opinions. Ownership causes disharmony among the team. It almost always gets in the way of finding the truth.
9. Contribute to maintaining a friendly atmosphere by speaking with courtesy, dignity, care, and moderation. This will promote unity and openness.
10. Aim at achieving consensus. If, however, consensus is impossible, let the majority rule. Remember, though, that decisions, once made, become the decision of every participant. Dissenting opinions are destructive to the success of the mission. When decisions are undertaken with total group support, wrong decisions can be more fully observed and corrected.

12.3 QUALITIES OF A TEAM PLAYER

The best way to discover the value of working in a group is by working with one. Teams are clear examples of how people with different functions cooperate and collaborate to achieve common goals that could not be attained by individuals. What team qualities do you bring to a group? What team qualities would you like to develop?

An effective team player. . .

- is flexible
- is mutual
- has a sense of humor
- meets deadlines
- volunteers
- asks for help
- has vision
- promotes the group
- networks with others
- summarizes
- celebrates team members' achievements
- is objective
- has positive energy
- is an active listener
- contributes ideas
- grows professionally
- carries through a project
- interprets data and information
- respects others
- informs the group
- remembers others
- acknowledges others' positive qualities

Football, a Team Model of Cooperation

A college football team provides a vivid analogy for observing two categories of roles that people assume in groups. Effective players are the ones who take responsibility for the task of moving the ball toward the goalpost, scoring points, and preventing the opponents from scoring. Their responsibilities are the basic and fundamental roles of passing, running, blocking, kicking, and tackling.

In a group, this activity is called task-oriented functions or roles. People who assume the task function initiate actions that help the group to get started and keep the process ongoing by starting the dialogue. They do this by seeking information, providing information and opinions, elaborating on information, coordinating ideas, organizing related ideas, summarizing, and testing the workability of ideas. All of the following task-oriented roles or functions will help a group to be successful:

1. *Initiating:* This person gets things started and introduces new ideas throughout the meeting.
2. *Seeking information:* This person asks, "What I want to know is. . ."
3. *Giving information:* This person provides facts and data about the topic being discussed.
4. *Clarifying:* This person clarifies what is being said by stating: "Let me understand what you said. Do you mean. . ."
5. *Summarizing:* This person provides a summary of what has been said.
6. *Checking for consensus:* This person asks, "Are we all in agreement that. . ."

Besides carrying out the fundamentals of the game, football team members provide spirit and encouragement for one another by slapping each other on the back, cheering each other on, hugging each other, and slapping each other's hands with a "high-five" gesture.

In other groups, those who fill these "spirit" or maintenance functions contribute to the group by encouraging others, harmonizing differences, relieving tension, and expressing a group feeling. They usually perform the following maintenance-oriented roles or functions:

1. *Encouraging:* This person provides emotional support.
2. *Gatekeeping:* This person quiets the individual who is monopolizing the conversation and invites the quiet members in the group to participate.
3. *Harmonizing:* This person brings together the ideas of two or more participants.
4. *Relieving tension:* This person uses humor to "lighten up" the discussion without derailing the process or calling undue attention to himself or herself.
5. *Expressing group feelings:* This person takes responsibility to identify and express emotions underlying a discussion or behind a decision.

Obstacles to Team Success

As in football or any team effort, if a player puts his own interest ahead of the team's interest, both the player and team experience less-than-desired results. When people are self-oriented in groups, they are counterproductive. They often block the process, seek recognition for themselves, dominate the group, pursue special interests, and avoid contact with others and the task.

People who have a **hidden agenda**—the desire to pursue a different process or outcome than has been publicly stated within a group—often disrupt the group process by raising their particular grievances or concerns or finding fault with any suggestions for improvement made by other group members. In this situation, the convener of the meeting and group members may want to acknowledge what is being said but remind the speaker that their meeting time needs to be focused on the group agenda.

Self-oriented blockers have their own agenda. Some agendas are more obvious than others, but it is important to be aware of what might be motivating a person's statements. Here are some clues to identify those times when a person is trying to sidetrack the group:

1. *Yes, but…:* This person objects to an idea because of a perceived obstacle.
2. *TINTI (The Issue's Not The Issue):* This person has a personal axe to grind and is using the group forum for self-interest.
3. *Complaining:* This person complains about having to be part of a group.
4. *Interrupting:* This person speaks while others are speaking.
5. *Obstructing:* This person passes notes, whispers, or physically disrupts the meeting.

6. *Deflecting:* This person is a "naysayer" who insistently points out why an idea or strategy will not work.
7. *Controlling:* This person maintains the attitude that he or she has the final answer and there is no room for debate about it.

Healthy and Unhealthy Control

Attempts to block ideas frequently come from a need to control situations or other people. Deepak Chopra, a physician and the author of *Ageless Body, Timeless Mind,* notes that healthy control means being "secure enough in yourself (meaning your worth, lovability, and achievements) that outside events do not threaten your coping skills. The unhealthy way is to manipulate people and events so your weaknesses and insecurities are covered over. You need to be honest with yourself to achieve the healthy process successfully; you need to know your limits in various situations, which ones make you feel weak and which ones bring out your strengths. Self-knowledge is an anchor that makes unpredictability tolerable."

Managing Excessive Control

Everyone defines "excessive" control differently, because the balance of controlling and letting go of controlling are different for each of us. Like any behavior, change begins when we change our minds. Recognizing the warning signs of excessive controlling behavior is one of the key managing tools. Therefore, making a decision to begin letting go of some control can be very productive. Let's suppose a car pulls in front of you when you are in a hurry. Can you let your anger go? Can you see you have no control over the other driver? Suppose an exam is canceled because a teacher is sick after you studied for weeks. Is this something you can change? Irritating incidents can provide practice for "letting go" of control.

Some people repeat meaningful words, phrases, or sentences to themselves to help them look at incidents differently. A common bumper sticker says, "Let Go and Let God." When faced with a controlling issue, some people say to themselves, "It doesn't matter" or "It's no big deal." Saying this and meaning it brings peace of mind. Seeing things from this perspective helps them to "let go" of the issue. A sign on a bulletin board reminds an employee, "Don't just do something, stand there." Observing a behavior of her son, a mother says to herself, "There is nothing more I can do in this situation." Understood appropriately, these messages help us to see that there are situations beyond our control, and there are situations where attempting to control is counterproductive.

Managing Conflict in Teams

Conflict is a natural corollary to team building among colleagues, for when people discuss, they often disagree. How can peers in groups manage conflicts? A few guidelines can be helpful:

1. Look at whether the issue is important in itself, or is indicative of underlying disagreement on another level.
2. Be clear about why you are in conflict.
3. **Paraphrase**—that is, restate the other person's ideas in your own words. This has two advantages: (a) it tells the person that you are actively listening; and (b) it enables him or her to modify anything that has not been stated accurately.
4. Disengage yourself on a personal level from the disagreement. The disagreement is usually not about you personally.
5. Calm down, take your time, and enable yourself to be in control of your feelings before you decide to raise a major conflict issue. Time is your best ally.
6. Articulate your viewpoint as well as your needs with as much openness as possible. If you are open to suggestions, you and others are more likely to feel heard. If you are open about your own needs and feelings, your expressed vulnerability will invite a reexamination of the issues on the part of the other.
7. Base your viewpoint on facts, data, statistics, examples, and whatever other sources of research you can find that represent rational information.
8. Look for ways that you and others can find common ground.
9. If you find that you can accept and understand an opposing viewpoint or a modification of it, all parties will benefit.
10. When you feel inclined to be verbally nasty, take a deep breath, ask for a break, and visualize how you would feel if the words you were about to express were directed at you. Do whatever works to stop you from saying things that will damage the relationship.
11. If the conflict begins to escalate and cannot be resolved, invite a third party to mediate.

■ TIPS FOR SUCCESS ■
Building Teams

1. Regularly express appreciation to team members.
2. Be patient with the extra time it often takes to reach decisions, because there will be more people committed to the final decision. The decision will also likely be better than if it is made by only one person.
3. Work to understand the different styles of your team members, and allow everyone to contribute.
4. Look for points of unity between you and your team members.
5. Ask for a third-party mediator if you have a conflict you can't resolve.
6. Recognize and accept responsibility for your role in the conflict.
7. Be open and creative with new possibilities for increasing teamwork and decreasing conflict.

SCENARIO FOR SUCCESS

Leon Harris was intent on getting his fellow team members to work together on a sales projection for year's end. He had been with Innovative Marketing for three years, and during the time he was there, his teammates never seemed to agree or finish their goals without one person taking on the bulk of the work. Rather than jumping into a formal meeting, Leon invited the five men and women and their spouses over to his house for dinner. They all seemed relaxed and animated. The following week, when the team met for initial planning, Leon offered to pull the statistics if the other members would collaborate and present the accompanying visuals and reports for management. At the next week's meeting, Leon thanked everyone for following through on their portion of the work. Their projection report was a hit at the meeting.

Questions for Discussion

1. What strategies did Leon instigate in developing a successful projection report for management?
2. What other strategies could he utilize for future projects that would contribute to further success?
3. What successes and failures have you had in getting individuals to work together as a team? In retrospect, what would you now do differently to be more successful?

ACTIVITIES FOR SUCCESS

Activity 1: Team Decision Process

This exercise looks at the dynamic of a classroom team, working together to reach a settlement on a given issue. Sit so each person in the class or group can be seen by everyone else.

Objectives: (1) To experience the dynamic of team decision making; (2) to observe the various roles each person plays in the team effort.

Procedure: Do as a whole class.

    Step 1: Begin by generating an issue that the class would like to address. Perhaps the class wants to offer a solution to a lack of sufficient parking spaces on campus, explore ways to encourage safety on campus, promote student activities, or offer ideas to solve some other issue.

    Step 2: Everyone writes down the issue on a piece of paper, keeping it available during the discussion.

    Step 3: Choose someone to be moderator for the discussion.

    Step 4: Discuss the issue for ten to fifteen minutes.

Step 5: Using the cooperation checklist below, make a note of the task and maintenance-oriented functions you performed during the discussion.

Cooperation Checklist

What functions did I fill in the group discussion?

Task-Oriented Functions	Maintenance-Oriented Functions
Initiating	Encouraging
Seeking information	Gatekeeping
Giving information	Harmonizing
Clarifying	Relieving tension
Summarizing	Expressing group feelings
Checking for consensus	

Step 6: At the end of the discussion, class members share their perception of the various task-oriented functions that each fulfilled and if they were effective or not. Do the same with maintenance-oriented functions.

Activity 2: Obstacles to Successful Team Functioning

Ideally, a group is composed of active listeners who make positive contributions to the discussion. Let's assume, however, that there may be one or two people in a group whose personal concerns supercede the team's goal.

Objectives: (1) To identify obstacles to a team's successful functioning; (2) to respond to perceived blocks in the process.

Procedure: Work in small groups.

Step 1: Discuss what might be the hidden agenda behind each of the following comments:
1. "That idea was tried a few years ago, and it didn't work. I don't think we should consider it again now."
2. "That department hasn't met its production quota since Hal Redmond joined the department."
3. "Let's all share our homework answers."
4. "I don't know why we are talking about quality control when the real problem is favoritism."
5. "I give forty hours plus overtime to this company. Now they want me to go to school, too."
6. "That fraternity is always making trouble."
7. "How can we restructure this department? We're just the workers."
8. "I'll collect the pencils—you go ahead and make a decision without me."
9. "Do what you want. It doesn't matter to me."
10. "Let's get this meeting over with. I have work to do."
11. "Yes, but it won't work because no one wants to do it the right way."
12. "You'll never convince me. I won't change my mind."

Step 2: As an active listener, how would you respond to each of the above comments?

Activity 3: Group Brainstorming and Decision Making

To understand how critical thinking can impact our lives, let's look at how it works in everyday living. Lorene, a thirty-four-year-old single mother of two, does not earn enough as a bank teller to adequately prepare for her children's future or her own. She knows she cannot depend on her ex-husband to share the responsibility for the children, a thirteen-year-old girl and an eleven-year-old boy. Lorene is fairly certain that her job is secure, but no advancement is likely unless she has more education and learns new skills. Moreover, she has always wanted a career in marketing. She is considering leaving the bank to work as a waitress, because she thinks she can earn more money and have enough flexibility in her schedule to attend college and reach her goal.

In order to make a good decision, Lorene needs to do some critical thinking. Imagine that Lorene invites you and three or four good friends over for coffee to consult about her options.

Objectives: (1) To brainstorm in small groups in order to identify options; (2) to assess options in relation to appropriate critical-thinking questions; (3) to draft a written document and plan of action.

Procedure: Work in small groups.

Step 1: Brainstorming entails tossing out ideas without evaluating them to achieve a creative flow. Afterward, decisions can be made as to the practicality and effectiveness of each idea. Use brainstorming to identify the many options open to Lorene. Record all suggestions, even if some seem silly or impractical. Remember that criticism of ideas stops creative flow, and sometimes very effective ideas are sparked by unusual ones.

Step 2: Group the ideas from your brainstorming. Decide which ideas best address the problem and which are most workable.

Step 3: List some critical questions and try to answer them. What are the main problems with Lorene's present job? Has she explored the bank's continuing education policies? Are there marketing opportunities at the bank? Whom in the organization can she approach for advice? What about health insurance and sick leave benefits in case of illness? Would the increase in salary as a waitress be worth the trade-off in benefits? What about her children? Can they share some household responsibilities to help Lorene? How can she include her children in the process? Are there any relatives or friends Lorene can count on to be with them in emergencies? What type of degree could Lorene explore? How can she find out what courses of study are available and what jobs will be "hot" by the time she finishes? What other questions should Lorene consider?

Step 4: After considering all of the critical questions, imagine that Lorene makes a decision. Write out the decision and outline a draft plan of action to fulfill the decision in clear, concise steps.

Step 5: Decide whether you have expressed the critical issues in your draft. If necessary, gather more evidence and information. Revise your plan of action to include new ideas, evidence, and information.

JOURNAL FOR SUCCESS

Journal Entry

Objective: To be aware of your role, speech, and actions in group/team situations.

Procedure: Respond to the following questions in your journal:

1. Have you participated in a peer review session in any of your classes or a peer performance evaluation in a job setting? What was comfortable? What was difficult? How did you deal with it? How would you deal with it differently another time?

2. Think of a time when you were part of a decision-making team. Were you able to fully support the final decision? What happened when you did? What happened when you didn't?

3. Think of a time when you worked on a project with a team. Were you more productive and creative as a team than you would have been on your own? Why or why not?

4. What do you admire about teams that seem to work well?

CHAPTER 13
Job Search Success

Follow your bliss.

—Joseph Campbell

To Learn and Understand

- What factors can support a successful job search?
- Which résumé format suits your employment needs?
- How can you be a successful interviewee?
- How do people find jobs?

13.1 JOB SEARCH CONSIDERATIONS

Tracey is a single, intelligent young woman who wants to be a lawyer. Right now she is enrolled at a community college. She supports herself with two jobs as a waitress. Recently Tracey had a computer programming project assignment, which she planned to finish on Thursday evening. The restaurant where she works called Thursday afternoon to say they needed her to work that night. She explained her situation and respectfully asked if they could get someone else. They said, "No, you have to come in." Tracey said she couldn't, and she lost her job.

Although Tracey's employers did not tell her they were letting her go because of her refusal to work, she believes it was the reason. As much as she regretted losing the job, she thought that she had made a wise decision. She had examined her alternatives and determined that completing her class project was more important to her than the job. She could get another job, but she could not risk failing the course. Tracey was clear about the goal she wanted to accomplish.

Tracey's decision may or may not have been the one that you would have made. The important point here is that you need to know your goals, what range of options you have, and how comfortable you are with ambiguity, because, despite the millions of words that have been published on the subject of finding a job, ultimately the decision is yours.

Why Work?

This question appears to have a simple answer. We work to earn money or other compensation for what we do. However, this simple and obvious answer belies the complexity of the work ethic. Over the centuries, the concept of why we work has been integrally tied to religious beliefs and societal dynamics. The Puritan work ethic, for example, was primarily responsible for the early development of the United States and the emergence of universal education.

People who are value-centered seek jobs that promote their beliefs and causes. People who look to their jobs for satisfaction and a sense of self-worth seek jobs that meet those needs. Others desire to be of service and select their jobs accordingly.

Some workers seek their identities in their jobs. Today, **workaholism**—the tendency to work excessively and not lead a balanced life—is a serious addiction that may lead to other imbalances in a person's life. There is a definite tendency in society today to identify people's worth with their jobs. Pursuit of the American Dream has elevated the importance of the job as the path to material success and well-being. Pulitzer Prize–winning playwright Arthur Miller explores the dynamic of a failed worker in *Death of a Salesman*—a failure that causes Willy, the salesman, to see himself as useless. At one point Willy's son Biff confronts his father: "You were nothing but a hard-working drummer [salesman] who landed in the ash can like all the rest." Willy believed his worth came from his success on the job and not from his own sense of self-respect.

At a gathering of strangers, often a common opening question is, "What do you do?" While being a way to start a conversation, this question also highlights the importance of jobs in our lives. The drawback to the emphasis on jobs is that knowing the occupation of a person may unfairly label or pigeonhole that person, thus perpetuating stereotypes. Women who stay at home to raise their children, for example, have been known to label themselves as "just" a housewife. A job in a specific profession may make a man or woman a desirable romantic "catch."

What we do for a living, then, is more complex than we may initially believe. So, it may be helpful to consider the following guidelines as you go through the job search process.

Successful Job Seeking

Know Yourself What are your talents, dreams, hopes, and inclinations? In what areas have you had work experience? What did you enjoy about your previous jobs? What would you prefer not to do? What are your strengths and weaknesses? How do you visualize yourself five years from now? Ten years from now? What goals do you want to have accomplished? If you are not able to answer each of these questions now, the answers will become clearer as you learn more, experience more, and take more of a proactive role in deciding your future. Usually a sense of a person's goals emerges gradually, gaining energy with time.

Connect with People Sometimes people ignore the obvious in their job searches. By talking with family, friends, and associates, they can build up a network of resources that may be helpful to them in the future. Let's take the example of Aaron, who wants to be an elementary school teacher.

In order to gain experience in his chosen field, Aaron volunteers at a local elementary school during his college breaks. He helps the teachers copy materials, supervises at recess, and acts as an aide in the early childhood center. Aaron's volunteer services are helping him to gain experience in his chosen field of work and to test whether this is really the area that he wants to pursue. He enjoys the time he has with the children in the classroom, and he is beginning to visualize himself as a successful teacher. His volunteering is time well spent. Additionally, when Aaron does get his degree, he may want to ask his colleagues and administrators for letters of recommendation, and he will be able to point to his volunteering as part of his work experience. Gradually, Aaron's dream is gaining energy, and he is on his way to achieving his goal.

A word of caution, however: When you volunteer your services, do it because it is a satisfying experience for you, and not only because it may lead to something else. Good things happen to people when they let go of the possible outcomes and live in the present.

Use the Internet The Internet has become a great resource for job seekers. It can offer Websites for résumés, career guides, job postings, résumé writing suggestions, employer research sites, and so on. If you don't have a computer in your home, most schools and libraries offer services to assist you from their locations. (See the discussion on using computers in Chapter 2.)

Use College Services In addition to using the Internet independently in your job search, your university career center can show you how to use the Internet with special emphasis on the local situation. The main purpose of such university career centers is to enable their students to obtain internships and full-time jobs. Most career centers have computer programs that students can use to develop a personal and professional **résumé**, a document that summarizes your work experience and qualifications, your education, and the qualities that would make you an excellent employee. They may also have personality, aptitude, or career-related tests to assist you.

To Find a Job, Get a Job This is an oversimplification with a kernel of truth: opportunities for job advancement often arise within a company as your employer sees the contribution you are making. An entry-level position may seem unrewarding at first; however, with time, you may be called upon to be a member of a committee or to design a special project or to work with another company because of your proven track record within the organization. Any job can be a stepping stone to advancement.

Philippe is originally from Haiti. He came to the United States, requesting and receiving political asylum. After being hired as an entry-level hotel worker for a major international chain, he proved himself to be responsible and professional about his work and began taking college classes at night. Within a year, he advanced to training other entry-level employees. While in this position, he learned of a job opening in Hawaii as a troubleshooter. He applied for and got the job. Now Philippe troubleshoots for hotels all over the world.

Explore Jobs That Have Value for You Vicki is a twenty-year-old with an associate's degree entering the full-time job market for the first time. She is willing to take an entry-level position because she knows that she needs the work experience. Colletta, a homemaker, is returning to work after raising her family. She would like to find a job where her previous work experience would be honored and where the employer would provide her with current training in her field.

Each person weighs various factors differently, depending on his or her life situation, so explore jobs that have value for you.

Remember: No Job Is Forever We know that during the course of our lives most of us will need to re-train for alternative careers because of industrial and organizational mergers, downsizing policies, and technology advances that replace people's jobs. In the area of telecommunications, for example, the number of telephone operators of one major company has declined by 30,000 over a ten-year period. In the construction field, production of one ton of steel, which formerly took 10.1 man-hours, takes 3.2 man-hours (as of 1998), according to the American Iron and Steel Institute.

In *Working*, Studs Terkel's acclaimed book of oral histories of working Americans of various ages and backgrounds, the author tells the story of Mike LeFevre, a married, middle-aged Chicago steelworker. LeFevre fears being let go, but he finds his job oppressive. Because he is the only support for his wife and two children, he feels stuck in his job and thinks he has no future. His demoralizing story is representative of many workers who are caught in the labyrinth of conflicting employment decisions.

Keep Current in Your Field Forward-looking companies and organizations realize that their employees need ongoing training and educational opportunities in order to keep current about trends and changes in their area of work. Employers who are willing to invest in workers by sending them to seminars, providing on-the-job training opportunities, or by offering tuition reimbursement for college are exhibiting confidence in their workers. Workers who take advantage of ongoing training are helping themselves and their company.

Paolo was passed over for a promotion at his company. He approached his manager, concerned that he had done something wrong. His manager explained that management liked his work but needed someone in the position who had at least an associate's degree. The manager was willing to have his budget cover 75 percent of the tuition for Paolo to attend college in the evenings, provided he agreed to work for the company for at least one year after he completed his degree. Paolo started attending night courses and got the next promotion.

Be Realistic About Your Abilities As you gain knowledge of yourself, you will more fully realize where your strengths and limits lie. It is not negative to acknowledge your limitations; in the recognition comes the power to change those limitations to strengths. For example, Sarah has cared for animals since she was a child. She has had a dog, and she has raised birds. However, it would be unrealistic for Sarah to promote herself as an expert on animal behavior. She would do herself and the veterinarian who is her prospective employer a disservice if she were to misrepresent her experience. Honesty and integrity are important components of the job search.

Realize That There Is No Perfect Job When it comes to jobs, and to life in general, you will sometimes need to make trade-offs. Whatever the trade-off, it is important that you be comfortable and peaceful about your decision. Take the example of Benita, a young woman from the Philippines who wanted to study graphic design. She needed to supplement her financial aid package with a part-time job. A factory near her home had an opening for an assembly line position that paid considerably more than minimum wage. She was hired for the job. All day, Benita screws fan blades on fans. The work is repetitive and not particularly fulfilling; however, two factors make the job an acceptable trade-off: the money and the location. Benita knows that this job is not forever and that she is helping herself to achieve her goal of becoming a graphic designer.

Be Positive and Persistent While this statement sounds like a cliché, it merits attention. Job seeking is active: that is, it takes not only physical energy to keep your résumé updated, send out résumés, check the Internet, and go on interviews, but mental energy as well. View each application for employment and each interview as further steps in the process of finding a job. While not all of those interviews will lead to employment, it is important to remember that employers are looking for a match just as you are. Not getting the job does not necessarily mean that you are lacking competence; it might simply mean that you did not match with the company's idea of who they want for a position. So, don't get discouraged, stay fresh. Keep a smile on your face, and know that finding a job *is* a job, and you are doing your best.

13.2 RÉSUMÉS AND COVER LETTERS

A résumé is a fact sheet that summarizes the kind of information your prospective employer needs to know about you, such as your educational background, credentials, work experience, skills and abilities, degrees, any awards or special recognition you have achieved, and, as mentioned earlier, any volunteering you have done. The primary purpose of a résumé is to "sell" you and your abilities well enough to obtain an interview. Its secondary purpose is to guide the interviewer in asking you questions. When done well, the process of creating a résumé can also build confidence in your abilities.

A résumé must be tailored to present your qualifications in the best manner possible. While there are many books and guidelines regarding résumé writing, it is important that you are satisfied with the way the document represents you and your potential. You must be able to honestly discuss all aspects of your résumé in an interview, so it is unwise to inflate or misrepresent yourself.

Many larger companies now have résumé-scanning software to help them review a large volume of résumés quickly to identify those of candidates most likely to merit an interview. The software is designed to spot key words in a résumé that indicate desired skills and industry-specific experience. Read job advertisements carefully to be certain that the skills they are looking for are reflected in your résumé. If possible, talk to someone in human resources in a similar company to learn what words are important to include. Ask a reference librarian to assist you with researching industry-specific terminology.

Companies often use their own Websites or others designed to post job opportunities and résumés to find candidates. Each Website has its own structure and process for posting your résumé and connecting with interested employers.

A hard-copy résumé for a beginning job seeker should be only one page. A professional with many years of experience might have one that is two or three pages long. Employers do not have time to read more than this.

Sample Résumés

Many resources are available to you in writing a résumé. If you want to write the résumé on your own, your library will have books showing samples of résumés for your reference. Professional consultants are also available to help you design your résumé. Free resources are often available from your college, government offices, or the Internet, as mentioned previously.

Karen S. Hoovler, a career consultant and school psychologist, offers the following information about résumés and supplies effective sample résumés. First, she explains, there are different résumé formats. If your target position is academia, a **curriculum vitae** or **chronological résumé** is generally expected; in other fields a **functional résumé** may be preferred.

In the curriculum vitae, or chronological résumé, your previous work experience is outlined, most recent first, with bullets detailing your responsibilities and accomplishments. This type is effective if you are looking for a position in the field in which you already have experience. If, however, your background and training are in education and you are interested in a position in public relations, this could be a detriment. In this case, a functional résumé, which emphasizes your transferable strengths and skills will be more successful.

Figure 13.1 illustrates a curriculum vitae/chronological résumé for Jesse Talem, a teacher who plans to stay in education but move into administration.

Figure 13.2 illustrates a functional résumé, another version of Jesse's résumé, which he is using to respond to the following ad for a public relations position.

Classified Ad

Public Relations

Successful Applicant: Works closely with marketing team with the assigned account groups to ensure consistent messaging to the media, and supports marketing and PR objectives. Drives direction and implementation of PR programs. Develops press campaigns and tactics. Builds measurability into programs by analyzing and reporting on efficacy of projects and campaigns. Initiates and maintains positive, productive relations with key media and industry. **Required Skills:** Bachelor's degree in communications, public relations, or related field. Resourceful multitasking work style. Strong written and oral communications skills. Ideal candidate will understand the product and target audience. Proficient in MS Word and WordPerfect; 3–5 years experience preferred.

JESSE TALEM

8917 Woodbridge Court	(H) 216-846-3395
Cleveland, OH 44107	(O) 216-229-1850

Jmt@coolmail.com

My objective is to secure an administrative position where I can utilize my management and educational leadership skills, developed over time in an elementary school setting.

EDUCATION

Master of Education
Administration
State University
2000

Bachelor of Science
Education
MIE University
1994

CERTIFICATIONS

Ohio State Department of Education	Elementary Principal
Ohio State Department of Education	Elementary (K–8)

CONFERENCES / SEMINARS

Phonemic Awareness
Phonics and Phonemic Awareness; Practical Strategies for Beginning Readers and Writers
Lifelong Literacy Begins in the Primary Grades
International Thespian Conference
State of Ohio High School Theatre Conference

MEMBERSHIPS / COMMITTEES

National Education Association
Ohio Education Association
Ohio Educational Actors Association – Board Member
Superintendent's Advisory Council
Continuous Improvement Plan Committee

(continued)

Figure 13.1 ■ Curriculum Vitae or Chronological Résumé

PROFESSIONAL EXPERIENCE

Elementary Teacher   1996 – Present
Wafer Heights City School

- **Designed database** for student demographics, academic progress, and academic awards and **instructed colleagues** in the use and implementation of this database.

- As part of a team effort, developed, wrote, and presented the building **Continuous Improvement Plan 2000**.

- **Wrote district-wide science curriculum** for kindergarten as well as participated in the writing of the **State of Ohio Actors Curriculum**.

- Served on building **Intervention Assistance Team**. Assessed present level of student functioning and designed interventions for remediation.

- **Revised** staff **handbook** outlining operations procedures and state and local policies.

- **Wrote and published** weekly parent **newsletter**.

- Responsible for **organizing and conducting yearly school-wide assembly**.

High School Theatre Director   1996 – Present
Wafer Heights City Schools

- Responsible for **budget administration**, **scheduling, and transportation** for theatre organization.

- **Chartered** International Thespian Troupe. **Organized** Parent Booster Organization.
- Composed **publicity and press releases** for high school theatre organization. Designed, wrote, and published 30+ page programs for each theatre production.

My **computer skills** include Macintosh Apple Works, PageMaker, Microsoft Word, and Corel WordPerfect as well as educationally specific software.

PERSONAL

In addition to my professional responsibilities, I am very active in my community. I am a member of the Community Booster Club and direct Summer Community Theatre.

POTENTIAL

My strong organizational and communications skills combined with my experience in the classroom and with parents will make me an asset to your administrative staff.

Figure 13.1 ■ *(continued)*

JESSE M. TALEM

8917 Woodbridge Court   (H) 216-846-3395
Cleveland, OH 44107   (W) 216-229-1850

Jmt@coolmail.com

My **energy**, **enthusiasm** and **dedication** to produce results coupled with strong **communication** and **organizational** skills are attributes I can bring to your firm in the area of:

PUBLIC RELATIONS

emphasizing

COMMUNICATIONS AND COMMUNITY RELATIONS

QUALIFICATIONS

- Highly skilled at **assessing** needs and developing **programs/curricula** to meet those needs, able to develop quality programs to **enhance understanding** and **appreciation** in target audiences.

- Exceptional ability to **manage, influence,** and **communicate** with individuals from all walks of life.

- Able to **conceptualize, develop,** and **execute** projects **on time** and **under budget**.

- Superior **organizational** and **time management skills**, organized, effective, and detail oriented.

- Proven **leadership** skills, able to conceptualize and **develop new programs** and foster their growth.

- Skilled in the use of a **team approach** to problem solving and in motivating others, able to wear "many hats" and handle **multiple tasks under pressure**.

- Outstanding **interpersonal** and **communication skills,** able to communicate with people at all levels of the organization.

- Proficient in Macintosh AppleWorks, PageMaker, Microsoft Word, and Corel WordPerfect, as well as utilizing educationally specific and scanner software.

CAREER SUMMARY

Wafer Heights City Schools **Teacher**	1996 – Present
Wafer Heights City Schools **Theatre Director**	1996 – Present
Evans Public Schools **Teacher**	1994 – 1996

(continued)

Figure 13.2 ▪ A Functional Résumé in Response to an Ad

SELECTED ACCOMPLISHMENTS

- **Founded theatre program** which became **recognized** at **local**, **state,** and **national** levels.

- **Prepared** and **administrated** yearly **budgets** for theatre seasons. Developed and implemented **fundraising activities**.

- Composed **publicity** and **press releases**. **Designed, wrote,** and **published** programs for each production.

- As member of State Board of the Ohio Educational Theatre Association, **created** theatre **curriculum, managed facilities** at state conferences, and **judged theatrical productions**.

- Lead **team effort** in developing, writing, and presenting **long-range improvement plan**.

- **Revised** educational **curriculum** to meet state and national guidelines.

- **Designed database** to track the progress of projects and events, and **instructed colleagues** in the use and implementation of this database.

EDUCATION

I received my Bachelor of Science in Education degree from MIE University of Ohio in 1994 and a Master of Education in Administration from State University in 2000 and hold a current Teaching Certificate and a certificate in School Administration. I have studied German for 5 years.

PROFESSIONAL AFFILIATIONS

State Board of the Ohio Educational Theatre Association
Educational Theatre Association
Ohio Theatre Alliance
International Thespian Society
Ohio Education Association
National Education Association

Figure 13.2 ■ *(continued)*

Cover Letters

A **cover letter** should always accompany a résumé that is mailed to a prospective employer. It introduces you to the employer and states your request to be considered for a position. Cover letters should include information about why and how you qualify for the particular job.

Figure 13.3 illustrates a letter that Jesse Talem might have sent along with his résumé responding to the classified ad on page 92. Notice how Jesse takes the requirements of the ad and fits them to his qualifications. The ad's requirements that do not fit Jesse's capabilities, he ignores—as, for example, the three to five years of public relations experience.

In addition to responding to classified ads, the savvy job-hunter looks for unadvertised opportunities. In this case, Jesse did a career search on companies for whom he believed he could make a significant contribution. One of them was Knew Learning Materials, to whom he wrote the cover letter shown in Figure 13.4 to accompany his functional résumé.

13.3 INTERVIEWING

Because meeting a prospective employer face-to-face for the first time can create anxiety, the better prepared you are for your job interview the easier the experience will be.

Before the Interview

Research the Organization Where You Will Be Interviewed The public library and your college career services department can assist you with obtaining information about businesses from reference books, news articles, and the Internet. If the company you are researching is a public corporation, you can call to ask for its latest annual report. Check the daily news for any references to the organization, and know its primary services or products. It is important to walk into an interview armed with as much information about the company as possible. It shows that you are serious about the company and that you are able to find information when you need it.

Investigate the Company Culture Each company has its own culture, and determining if you are a good fit with it or not can be key to being successful on a job. To understand the culture, talk to current and former employees and members of professional trade associations to which the company's employees belong. You can look in annual reports for stories about company "heroes" to see what is valued in performance.

Prepare a List of Questions to Ask the Employer Having a list of detailed questions will show the interviewer that you researched the company and have an interest in it. Ask questions about projects the company is involved in, profits/losses, long-term goals, mission statement, company training programs, and other relevant issues. Some questions you can ask during an interview to learn about the culture might include the following: What is the company's mission? How does the company communicate with its employees? Does the company encourage employees to learn more about the business? How do people get feedback? How do executives expect to be addressed? What is the company's dress code? What are typical work schedules? How are decisions made? How are raises and promotions decided? Who are the star performers, and how are they achieving their goals?

Review Your Answers to Key Questions That the Interviewer Is Likely to Ask Questions you might be asked include the following:

- *What do you know about our company?* This is an opportunity to compliment the interviewer regarding the company. Do your research ahead of time, and be specific.
- *Tell me about yourself.* Have a 1 to 1½ minute response prepared. Include education and work experience. Avoid offering personal information unless it is relevant to the position.
- *Why do you want this job?* Talk about why you think it is a good fit for you.
- *What contribution can you make to the job?* Briefly describe how you can meet the needs of the company.
- *What qualities do you bring to the job?* Provide two or three qualities that you have that are relevant to the position, then ask what qualifications they are looking for in someone in that position. File these away in your mind and include examples from your experience that demonstrate the qualifications throughout the interview; suddenly you may become just the person for whom they are looking.
- *What experiences will help you to succeed in this job?* Be specific but keep your story brief.
- *What are your strengths and weaknesses?* When discussing a weakness, choose a strength and make it sound like a weakness. Example: "I am a very organized person, and sometimes I tend to get frustrated when I am working with people who are not as organized as I am."

JESSE M. TALEM

8917 Woodbridge Court
Cleveland, OH 44107

(H) 216-846-3395
(O) 216-229-1850
Jmt@coolmail.com

April 4, 2004

Ms. Karen Brady
Vice President, Public Relations
Knew Learning Materials
6414 Hone Parkway
Cleveland, OH 44139

Dear Ms. Brady,

Recently, I have been conducting research to identify learning materials companies where I could make a significant contribution in Communication and Public Relations. During the course of this research, I identified your company. I believe that you would want to be aware of my interests and availability, and I am very interested in learning of your needs.

I offer proven skills, competencies, and experience including:

• Ability to identify needs of target audiences and ensure a message consistent with these needs.

• Superior written and oral communications skills developed in an educational environment.

• Strong organizational skills; ability to handle multiple tasks under pressure.

I am confident that a personal meeting will be of mutual interest and benefit.

While you are reviewing my qualifications, please note that I will contact your office next week. I will be happy to discuss any questions you may have at that time and the possibility of setting up an introductory meeting.

I look forward to speaking with you.

Sincerely,

Jesse M. Talem

Jesse M. Talem

Enclosure

Figure 13.3 ▪ A Cover Letter for an Unadvertised Opportunity

JESSE M. TALEM

8917 Woodbridge Court
Cleveland, OH 44107

(H) 216-846-3395
(W) 216-229-1850
Jmt@coolmail.com

February 15, 2003

Mr. Luke Prentice
Vice President, Public Relations
Shaffer Information Services
1050 Burywood Drive, Suite 16
Atlanta, GA 30338

Dear Mr. Prentice:

As a young energetic professional with exceptional skills in the area of public relations and communications, I am writing to you about your Public Relations position.

I am confident that my skills and professional attitude will make me an ideal candidate to promote Shaffer Information Services.

YOUR REQUIREMENTS	MY QUALIFICATIONS
Work closely with marketing teams	Led team effort in writing and presenting the plan for a new organizational direction.
Develop press campaigns and tactics	Designed publicity campaigns and all press releases for organization.
Have strong written and oral communications skills	Six years of experience in teaching and demonstrating theatre and other platform skills. Published numerous documents, brochures, and articles.
Resourceful multitasking workstyle	Able to handle multiple tasks under pressure.

As requested, I have enclosed my résumé with further details of my qualifications and accomplishments. I look forward to meeting with you to discuss how I may fit into your organization.

Sincerely,

Jesse M. Talem

Jesse M. Talem

Enclosure

Figure 13.4 ▪ A Cover Letter in Response to an Ad

In answering the questions, provide a specific picture of your positive qualities. Go beyond saying the obvious, such as, "I am always on time" or "I always give 100 percent." Punctuality and serious intention are assumed. What do you have to offer that is unique, creative, and outstanding? You may want to refer to the results of any personality or career tests you have taken. Consider projects to which you contributed significant ideas, and plans that you have implemented. You might even prepare a folder of outstanding accomplishments that represent you positively. Bring along any letters of recommendation that have been written on your behalf, or bring a neatly word-processed list of references that the employer may contact.

One way to describe a strength is to think of the acronym STAR (provided by Annie Heidersbach, Director of Career Services at Baldwin-Wallace College):

- **S**ituation
- **T**ask
- **A**ction
- **R**esult

Recall three to five situations in your experience where you can briefly describe what was going on, what needed to be done, what you did, and the outcome. Showing a prospective employer that you had this experience leads them to understand more of your abilities and accomplishments than just what is listed on your résumé.

Keep in mind that people tend to remember stories better than dry narrative. When employers are considering several applicants, a story may lead to a scenario like this: "Oh, I remember her! She was the one who came into the retail site that had lost money for three consecutive quarters, and she turned things around in just one month by simply redesigning the floor plan and reassigning staff to sales-generating activities."

Be Prepared to Describe How You Would Handle a Work Scenario Many employers present real-life scenarios that the prospective employee is likely to face on the job and require answers about how to handle them. To prepare ahead of time, pose questions for yourself that might be a challenge to answer, such as, "What would you do if you and another employee differed about how to do a project?" or "What would you do if you were asked to work overtime?" Reflect on the answers you want to provide.

Set Up a Mock Interview Ask someone whose position somewhat matches that of the interviewer to role-play an interview with you prior to the actual interview. Again, your college may have people who could do this with you and give you feedback on how you come across, so you can improve and be better prepared for the "real thing." You may even find it helpful to videotape the practice interview so you can review your performance. This simulation shows you where you need to put additional emphasis, or add information.

Confirm That You Know the Correct Time and Place of the Interview If the location is not familiar, check the directions you were given against a map and drive to the location in order to ascertain how much time you will need to get there punctually. Come prepared with a briefcase of your materials, including at least four copies of your résumé to give interviewers, and paper and a pen for taking notes. If the interview is out of town, arrive the day before and familiarize yourself with the area.

Dress Appropriately for the Interview Dress will vary, depending on the job you are seeking. If you will be in an office, business attire is appropriate: tie and jacket for men; a dark-colored suit or tailored dress for women. If the interview is for a less formal position, dress may be casual. Whatever the attire, you will want to be neat and clean. This includes checking your nails to be sure they are clean and trimmed, and seeing that your shoes and briefcase are presentable and your coat free of cat or dog hairs. Even if the employees of a company dress casually, it is important for an interviewee to be dressed more formally.

At the Interview

Arrive Early Arrive at the location early for the appointment so you can prepare yourself, relax, and take in the work environment. Do not arrive at the interviewer's office more than ten minutes before your interview. It gives the impression that your time is not valuable and you are just hanging around. If you are not absolutely sure of the spelling of the interviewer's name, take time when you arrive to ask the receptionist for that information. This is important since you will want to send a follow-up thank-you note. The interviewer will also likely give you his or her business card.

Take Documents Take information with you about the educational institutions you have attended, including transcripts, as well as full information about employers and references. The information needs to contain full names, addresses, and phone numbers. The references need to be on a separate sheet and contain three to five names. Make certain that the references indicate the relationship of the person to you and that they are on stationery that matches your résumé. Don't use best friends! The most effective references are from people such as former work associates, coaches, teachers, student group advisors, religious leaders, and community involvement colleagues. Be sure that your references know you are using their names and are prepared to speak positively about you if they are contacted.

Exercise Self-Control When you are introduced to the interviewer, greet him or her with a firm handshake and a smile. Be sure you have good eye contact. If you have a résumé, letters of recommendation, and so forth, offer them at this time. From then on, let the conversation be led by the interviewer, but make it a two-way conversation. Sit up straight in the chair. Take some slow, deep breaths to relax yourself. Listen attentively and maintain eye contact as the interviewer presents the requirements of the job. You may be eager to speak; resist interrupting. You will have an opportunity to speak when the interviewer asks you questions.

Match Your Energy Match your energy with that of the interviewer. Be yourself, but do not be overly loud or abrasive. An interviewer may want to start out with an informal chat in order to put you at ease and to become comfortable with you. So, the conversation may go to the weather, how long it took you to get there, and so forth. This opening informality is usually intended to be short. In any case, go with the flow of the conversation.

Communicate Clearly When the interviewer opens the conversation with you, speak clearly, distinctly, and in a focused manner. Don't "babble" on and on. Answer the question and elaborate as you need to for the interviewer to get a true picture of your potential for the job. Let your words reflect your discipline and integrity. You are worthwhile and will be an asset to the job; otherwise, you would not be at the interview. Let your manner reflect your confidence in yourself. At the same time, know that hiring is always somewhat of a risk, even with the most impeccable credentials, for people's personalities can only be truly experienced in the day-to-day work environment. So, appreciate the employer's desire to be thorough, and answer questions as completely as you can.

Ask Questions In the unlikely situation where the interviewer does not open the conversation with you, you may have to directly say that you have some questions, and then proceed. Ask for a specific job description, if one has not been offered to you. Take time to read it thoughtfully. If there is an area with which you are not familiar, indicate your willingness to train for it. If the interviewer asks you to provide further information, take a test, or fill out an application, indicate your willingness to comply, and take down any information that you will need to know in order to carry out the request.

Ask when the interviewer anticipates that the position will be filled. If she replies, "We should be making our decision by the end of the week," then ask, "If I haven't heard from you by say, Wednesday of next week, may I call you?" Never leave the situation vague as to how you will know whether you were accepted. If you have another job offer, be honest in saying that you do and that you need to know by a particular date. Ask any other questions that are important for you to know in making a decision should the job be offered to you; however, avoid asking about salary or benefits unless the interviewer raises these subjects first. If this happens, avoid a direct answer if possible. Remember "he who talks about money first loses." Should you be asked directly about your financial needs, you might respond by saying something like, "Although money is important, what is most important is that we have a good fit. Could you tell me more about . . ." then ask a question that would clarify expectations or requirements. If the interviewer persists regarding money, give an expected range; for example, "mid-to-high thirties." Don't discuss details of money until an offer has been made. If there are any constraints or concerns that you need to discuss, now would be the time to do that. The interviewer will appreciate your responsibility and honesty in raising such questions at this time.

Understand Promises In a rare case, an interviewer may make a statement such as, "You would probably be promoted within the year" or "We might want you to take on this new responsibility once you establish yourself." Clarify such statements to be sure that you understand correctly whether they are clear promises or simply possibilities.

Close Courteously At the end of the interview, close courteously, thanking the interviewer for the time he or she has given to you. Indicate that you are interested in and qualified for the position. Let the interviewer know that you are available by phone at the numbers listed in case there are further questions.

After the Interview

Plan a Courteous Follow-up Immediately after the interview, mail an appropriate thank-you letter to the interviewer(s). This is important even if you are not interested in the position. It leaves the possibility open for a different position with the company or for them to refer you to another prospective employer. If you have additional information to provide, you may include it in the letter. This should be a typed letter, not a handwritten note. Affirm why you want the position and believe you are well suited to it.

Relax . . . But Call Until you are notified of the decision, let go of the possible outcomes, since the decision is now out of your control. If you don't hear anything from the employer after the date that was mentioned, it would be appropriate to call and inquire whether a decision has been made. Make sure you have a plan to remind you to follow up with the company, especially if you are doing multiple interviews in a short period of time.

Evaluate the Interview Take time to write a few notes about key things that happened in the interview. Assess your interview answers and behavior to see if there are areas that need improvement and practice.

13.4 JOB SEARCH RESOURCES

There are a number of paths to employment, and it makes sense to try all of them. The choices you have include the following:

1. Apply directly to an employer in person, through the mail, or through the company's Website (which often lists job openings).
2. Ask friends and relatives for referrals to people they know are hiring.
3. Read and answer newspaper advertisements. Be aware of special newspapers just for job seekers or days that the newspaper runs more ads.
4. Use private employment services or recruiters.
5. Use government job centers.
6. Use school placement services.
7. Attend job fairs to meet prospective employers.
8. Put your résumé on both general job search Websites like **www.monster.com** or industry-specific ones, which you can find by doing an Internet search.

Using the maximum number of options increases your opportunities for being hired successfully.

Government Resources

Civil service jobs are available throughout the U.S. government, whose offices are listed in the phone book under "U.S. Government." Civil service jobs require that applicants take a test in order to be considered for the open positions. Written and performance tests are given in such areas as verbal ability (grammar, spelling, language use); reading comprehension; judgment, communication, observation, and memory skills; mechanical aptitude; clerical ability; arithmetic ability; as well as in subject-specific areas. Sample tests may be obtained through your local library and often through your university as well. States and cities each have additional resources for job placement and retraining. Check with your university, local libraries, or governmental offices for information and assistance.

Civil service jobs are available to U.S. citizens in dozens of areas such as the following:

Park ranger	Secretary	Nursing	Librarian
Police	Computer specialist	Pharmacy	Immigration
Social services	Telecommunications	Engineering	Food inspection
Salary and wage administration	Soil conservation Accounting	Workers' compensation Agriculture	Transportation Safety
Labor relations	Tax examining	Building management	Air traffic control

University and Library Resources

Your university may have a bulletin board or career center with resource material and current job openings. The counselors at your college can also provide you with information. Many colleges have aptitude and skills placement tests, in case you are not sure what career you want to pursue. Schools also sponsor job fairs, where local company representatives come to the school with information regarding a variety of positions. This is a good opportunity to explore several possibilities within a short period of time. Employers sometimes call individual departments of schools for referrals of students who might want to work for them. Departments will pass along this information to students.

Colleges and local libraries provide books, pamphlets, and interlibrary loan resources on job search information. Annual reports of companies are usually available in the reference area of the library. Information is available on over 10,000 companies, with descriptions of businesses, net sales, and so forth.

Directories of U.S. companies are available through the *D & B [Dun & Bradstreet] Million-Dollar Directory*, *Standard and Poor's Register of Corporations,* and *Corporate Affiliations*. These directories provide the name and address of a company, the nature of its business, and other basic information. The *International Directory of Company Histories* is a six-volume set that provides four- to six-page histories of over 1200 companies arranged by industry. *Hoover's Handbook of American Business* provides a brief overview and history of the company along with some financial information, and further information is at <www.hoovers.com>. Consult the career center at your college and the librarians at the reference desk for additional resources. Some corporations even have their own libraries and may allow you to do research there.

Other Possibilities

Temporary and part-time employment agencies train their clients in various fields, notably in basic computer skills, in order to make them marketable. It is not uncommon for employment agency clients to be moved from temporary to permanent status by a business after the employer has seen that the employee is a serious, responsible worker.

Don't rule out the possibility of creating your own position. Look for possibilities in the business section of your local newspaper or weekly business publication. If you read that XYZ Company is expanding their local operations or a business is relocating near you, find out who the decision maker is and write a letter explaining how you can help.

Informational Interviews

An informational interview can provide a wide range of information to a student about to graduate. If you are unsure of the type of company you want to work for or the responsibilities required of a type of position, an alumnus of your university with experience in your field may be willing to spend a brief amount of time with you to share this information. The alumni department can help you locate an appropriate person.

When setting the appointment, make it clear that the interview is for information only and that you have no expectation of employment. Limit the time to a maximum of thirty minutes unless the person offers more.

Research the company just as you would for a job interview. Prepare a list of questions aimed at what you need to know. You will likely ask more questions than the person will, since you are not being screened for a job with the company.

Dress and present yourself just as you would for an actual job interview. The company may consider you for a job at some point or refer you to another company, so you will want to make a positive impression.

Close the interview by saying thank you and ask for referrals to other people who could be sources of information. Send a thank-you letter acknowledging the person's time and help.

■ TIPS FOR SUCCESS ■
Job Search

1. Send a thank-you note after every interview, positively highlighting one or two specific items discussed.
2. Stay in regular contact with past advisors, employers, and professors who know you and your work and could be helpful to you in finding job leads.
3. Make sure people in your life have your résumé and ask for their assistance on your behalf. Give them at least two weeks' notice if you ask them for recommendation letters.
4. Practice interviews with a friend, associate, or counselor at your college.
5. Update your résumé regularly and send it out, even after you have secured a job. Sometimes the best opportunities come when you are not looking for them.

SCENARIO FOR SUCCESS

Alicia Samovar is looking for a position as a teacher in a top-notch school system. Jobs are scarce, and she is not having much success. One day she contacts the principal of the school she most wishes to work for and offers to work as a teacher's assistant as an unpaid volunteer for a two-week period. Her offer is accepted. Each day she works to make herself indispensable to the teacher. Every task she could do and every task she could learn from, she does. Shortly before her two weeks are complete, the class teacher falls on the sidewalk of the school, breaks her hip, and decides to retire. Alicia gets the opportunity to interview for the position.

Questions for Discussion

1. What strategy did Alicia effectively use to achieve her goal of employment?
2. Where do you think you could volunteer that would enable you to learn more about the kind of job in which you are interested?
3. What other things could you do to secure employment?

ACTIVITIES FOR SUCCESS

Activity 1: Visualization

Visualizing the job you want helps to define your specific career goals and how you can achieve them.

Objectives: (1) To visualize in detail a specific job you want to have; (2) to consider how you can make that visualization a reality.

Procedure:

Step 1: If this visualization is done in class, make yourself comfortable. If it is done at home, sit in your favorite chair at a time when you will not be interrupted. Play appropriate music in the background if you like. It is recommended that you either speak your visualization into a tape recorder or write it out for yourself. In this way you can more easily recall the visualization and repeat it daily until it becomes a natural part of your life.

Step 2: The following questions are offered as starters into the visualization:

1. Describe the location of where you are employed. Are you in an office? At home? Outside? In a building? What is the location like? What do you see? Hear? Smell? Touch?
2. What are you doing? Are you reading some important information you have just received? Are you talking with a patient? A client? A student? Are you closing an important deal? Are you comforting someone who has lost a loved one? Have you just made an important discovery? What is it? Why is it important? How will it be of value to others?
3. How are you personalizing your visualization? Are there diplomas and certificates on your office walls? Are there letters from grateful people? Are you reading about yourself in the newspaper or hearing about yourself on the news? Are others honoring you at a recognition dinner? Are your family and friends smiling at your accomplishments? Are you offering advice to others? What is that advice? Are you pleasantly relaxing, recalling the effects of your good services to others? Are you buying a new home or a luxury item that you have wanted? Do you see your children graduating from college as a result of your endeavors?
4. Read about your career accomplishments in your obituary. What is the headline? What did you accomplish in your life, according to the article? How did you influence others? How were you an outstanding citizen? How did you contribute to the happiness of others? What were your interests and pet projects?
5. What else do you visualize?

Step 3: In what ways did this visualization help you to focus on your desired career? Are you aware of steps you want to take to make the visualization a reality? List these steps.

Activity 2: Cover Letter and Résumé Writing

Written communications play an important part in letting people know your qualifications for a job. The cover letter is a way of highlighting the credentials that you want the employer to note and also provides you with an opportunity to supplement your résumé. The résumé itself is designed to promote you as a candidate with the qualifications needed for the position you are seeking.

Objectives: (1) To gain skill in writing a résumé and cover letter; (2) to match the information in the résumé with the job description of the position.

Procedure:

Step 1: Make an outline of the highlights of your education, work experience, excellent skills, and other significant information. Decide how you want to group this information: Chronologically? By experience? A combination? Be able to account for each year in some positive way. Whether you mention a short-term part-time job depends on the value you see in the job as it helps you to establish yourself in the résumé. The skill of résumé writing comes in selecting what is most relevant and significant from all the information you may have. You may have to decide to eliminate some information, such as earlier experiences in your job career, unless those experiences reinforce the progress you have made in your job experience. You may want to set up an appointment with the career counselor at your college to help you make your decisions. Be sure to quantify your experience if possible. For example, "increased sales by twenty percent in a three-month period" or "decreased costs by ten percent by. . . ."

Step 2: Obtain feedback from others in the class.

Step 3: Organize the résumé and prepare it for word processing.

Step 4: Set up your own résumé on a computer. Experiment with various font styles and spacing until you are satisfied with the result. For a hard-copy résumé, allow for sufficient "white space." Don't make your résumé too "busy" or the font too small. Employers don't want to struggle to read it.

Step 5: Write an appropriate cover letter to a prospective employer. Include how you became aware of the position, special features of your experience that you wish to highlight, and why you feel qualified for the position being offered. Follow the sample formats provided in this chapter.

Activity 3: Starting Your Job Search

Objectives: (1) To learn to use the Internet in your job search; (2) to test the effectiveness of your résumé.

Procedure:

Step 1: Post your résumé and complete your profile on <**www.monster.com**>.

Step 2: Monitor how often someone views your résumé and how often you are contacted by a potential employer.

Step 3: Review your résumé and make any necessary changes to increase the likelihood that an employer will read it.

JOURNAL FOR SUCCESS

Journal Entry

Some people take a relaxed view toward the job-seeking process, letting opportunities unfold for them. While this approach has merit, it is also important to set your own priorities for job choices.

Objectives: (1) To discover the aspects of job selection that are important to you; (2) to assess the kind of job you prefer based on the assessment.

Procedure:

Step 1: Answer each of the following questions briefly without dwelling on the answer. Just write down what comes to mind first.

1. Under what conditions would you stay in a job where you are not appreciated?
2. Would you be willing to give up a comfortable job in order to take a more exciting job that might involve relocating to another city or country? Answer the same question with regard to a higher salary. Explain your answer.
3. All factors being equal, how would you rate each of the following in terms of deciding whether to accept a job? Let the most important factor be #1, the next most important factor #2, and so on. Give #11 to the least attractive job characteristic.

_____ Interesting; in chosen field
_____ On-the-job training available
_____ Salary meets needs
_____ Potential for advancement
_____ Personal values reflected in company values
_____ Location is convenient and attractive
_____ Benefits meet needs
_____ Hours are a fit with lifestyle
_____ Management style compatible
_____ Rewards and incentives are generous
_____ Travel opportunities are available

4. If you had the opportunity to accept the job you really want, but it was a part-time job, would you accept it?
5. Most people want a job that provides some sense of satisfaction. What kind of job would you find satisfying? Why?
6. If you found a job that you really would like to accept, what trade-offs would you be willing to make? Explain.

Step 2: Discuss your answers with your classmates. What similarities and what differences do you notice? Has your discussion prompted you to reevaluate any of your answers? Explain.

Step 3: Based on your answers to the previous questions, write a brief summary in your journal of your job priority assessment.

CHAPTER 14

Success at Work

Companies that break spiritual laws, that lack love, integrity, justice, and respect, will over time show negative effects in some way. They may be initially successful, or even successful for quite a while, particularly if they have clever managers or little competition. However, the results of lovelessness, injustice, and disrespect will eventually make the organization less productive than it might have been.

—Dorothy Marcic

To Learn and Understand

- What is the difference between explicit and implicit norms?
- What are pivotal, relevant, and peripheral norms? What are some examples of them?
- Which work practices support success?
- What can you do to gain raises and promotions in your present organization or one that you may join in the future?

14.1 AWARENESS OF ORGANIZATIONAL CULTURE

No single methodology exists for being successful on the job. That said, normally one is expected to be competent or potentially competent and understand the workplace operation and culture. To be potentially competent and eventually to be capable of doing the job as expected by management, you need to be open to learn and willing to be trained. You also need to wake up and be aware of how the organization succeeds or fails.

Every organization has its own culture. It takes time for a new employee to understand both the written and unwritten rules. Some have very "open" policies, where employees are kept informed of major organizational happenings, managers' doors are largely open to employees, and new ideas are welcomed. Others are almost "closed," where keeping secrets is valued, innovation is rare, and growth is stagnant. Most organizations lie somewhere in between. It is important to understand in what kind of culture you can function at your best. You may need to work in a variety of settings before you determine this. Upon entering your new place of work, the key is to be aware. Observe what those on the fast-track are doing to move up, to gain recognition, and to increase responsibility, and, thus, to contribute more effectively to the mission of the organization.

In your awareness, note what and how things are being done; observe what appears to be important and what is not, what is being rewarded and what is not. Be interested and look for methods to improve the process and ways for your work to go beyond the minimum requirements. Do more than what is expected of you. Anticipate and satisfy the needs of management and of your coworkers. Enthusiasm counts, and smiling is one sign of your enthusiasm.

Written and Unwritten Norms

Norms—the rules of how to behave—are ubiquitous—that is, they are all over the place. They reveal what you need to know to be successful in your new place of work. **Explicit organizational norms** are often published in an organization's employee handbook. Further explanations are given at orientation programs and in company directives. Your manager and coworkers may offer additional advice. Pay attention and take these norms seriously, not only the first day on the job but every day.

Besides understanding these explicit norms, look for **implicit norms.** These are behaviors that you are expected to be aware of and follow, even though, for whatever reason, they are not publicly expressed.

Here's an example to illustrate implicit norms. When the 5 o'clock whistle blows announcing the close of the workday, almost immediately hourly workers scramble to leave the premises. As the human resources manager and a visitor stand at the door to her office, an employee dressed in business attire walks quickly past her door. She asks, "Do you see that fellow in the business suit going out the main entrance?"

"Yes," the visitor replies, turning his head to get a better look at him. "He will never make it in this organization," she states, confident in her prediction, "because he is leaving on time. In this organization, nobody who works in the office leaves at exactly 5 o'clock. They finish what they are doing, straighten up their desks, and then go home."

The visitor nods, indicating that he understands her meaning.

"And did you notice that he was not carrying a briefcase?" she asks. "That is another reason he will not make it here. Everybody leaves with their briefcases."

Of course, no one—other than the individual employee—knows whether or not the briefcase is ever opened. Nowhere in the employee handbook is it written that office employees are required to remain after 5 o'clock. In fact, the opposite is recorded—namely, that they are free to leave at 5 P.M. They are also not instructed to take their briefcases home with them. Both practices, however, are implicit norms of this company.

Office employees who leave after 5 P.M. and carry their briefcases out with them are perceived by management to be motivated team players worthy of **promotion** to a higher level of responsibility. Office employees who do not follow these unwritten rules are viewed as unmotivated non-team players and will not be promoted and, perhaps, will not even retain their jobs.

Attending company holiday parties or picnics is viewed similarly in this organization. Individuals who are aware of the importance of these events and desire to remain employed for the long term put in an appearance and at least behave like they enjoy the parties—without drinking too much or talking too loudly.

Ask yourself whether there are any such implicit norms operating where you work. Wake up and look around. They may be part of the reason you have not been promoted, given raises, or given greater responsibility at work, even though you think you deserve it.

Edgar H. Schein, an organizational psychologist, has identified three types of norms: (1) pivotal, (2) relevant, and (3) peripheral. **Pivotal norms** have to do with the very integrity of the organization. Failure to follow such norms leaves the organization no alternative but to let the person go. Examples of violating pivotal norms (and laws!) in many organizations are activities such as using illegal drugs, stealing, sabotage, acts of violence, and disclosing trade secrets or confidential information outside the company. For example, an employee who regularly buys supplies for a spouse's home office and puts them on an expense account will probably lose his or her position, because stealing breaks a pivotal norm.

Relevant norms are behaviors that can lead to promotion, such as appearance or volunteering to do more than is expected of you. Section 14.2 offers specific steps that lead to success on the job, which when ignored, can result in one's failing to qualify for promotion and raises in many organizations.

Peripheral norms are minor infractions such as returning late from lunch. Schein suggests that breaking these does not result in serious or significant consequences for the norm breaker. A slight reprimand or negative feedback from a coworker is all that is likely to occur. You learn that you have made a mistake and need to improve.

Organizations with few rules and regulations or threats of severe consequences tend to be more effective in today's environment. Employees are encouraged to do whatever it takes within the law and constraints of respect for customers, suppliers, and coworkers to get the job done. Employers reward proactive, creative activities on the part of their employees and expect them to learn from their mistakes. This type of management understands that punishment results in fearful employees who are reticent to take risks and try new approaches. Under those conditions, managers are left to do all the thinking, which is a poor use of human resources. Hence, within enlightened organizations, creative individualists find better ways of servicing customers by breaking ineffective peripheral norms and norms no longer relevant or even pivotal, and cut through red tape to simplify work processes, making the organization ever more flexible and effective.

Becoming aware, therefore, is not simply paying attention to the norms of the organization, as important as this is, but also thinking through the implications of these norms and acting accordingly. In so doing, the situation becomes a win-win situation for you and your company. As the organization succeeds, those responsible for its success also succeed.

14.2 IMPORTANT NORMS FOR SUCCESS

Many organizations have some unique expectations that grow out of their own history. Nearly all organizations, however, have certain norms that are part of the larger culture in which they live. Dressing and behaving appropriately, having a good attitude, being open to learning, and having other qualities that make for good citizens in any environment can help you reach the level of success you are aiming for in your career.

Be Aware of Your Appearance

1. *Be appropriate.* Think about how many judgments you make about your friends and family simply by looking at them. The same thing happens on the job. Even where casual dress is acceptable, how casual you look could cause people to make assumptions about you. If your hair is always messy or your shoes rarely polished, how careful could you be about the quality of your work? If your clothes look like you slept in them for three days, do you really respect and value your job, company, or coworkers? Neatness counts. So does cleanliness.

2. *Observe dress codes.* Many companies in the United States have adopted relaxed dress codes. It is common to find places where casual dress is acceptable at least one day a week. Often, however, it is important to distinguish between casual social wear and casual business dress. Many companies will not allow jeans with holes, T-shirts, or exercise-type clothing.

3. *Consider your future.* As you dress in the morning, it is important to consider who will see you that day. Will you present a professional image of yourself and the company to visitors? If they are in business suits, and you are in jeans, will it affect the balance and respect of your interaction? If you are giving a presentation to a group of coworkers, will dressing up give a little boost to your confidence? Will you be in a situation where someone who affects a potential promotion will be present? A good guideline is to look your best and dress for the job you want rather than the job you have.

Toby Chancellor was an administrative assistant to a marketing manager for an international electronics manufacturer. He knew he wanted to be a customer service representative; however, he noticed that people in that position ordinarily dressed in business suits. He stopped wearing casual clothes to work and dressed for his goal. When he received a promotion a few months later, his new manager commented on his ability to present a professional image to customers.

Be Aware of Your Attitude

1. *Have a service attitude:* Your job security depends on how well you serve your customers, both internal and external. You are responsible for adding value to these relationships. A customer is anyone to whom you provide

service in the course of your work. Internal customers are those who work for the same company as you, but usually in different departments. Their jobs are partly dependent upon your service to them for their success. External customers are other individuals or companies that are dependent upon your goods or services to be successful. The better the relationships you build, the higher the quality of service. The more you anticipate their needs, and the faster you respond to their needs, the more likely you will keep them as customers. Service is a key factor in staying competitive. And a positive service attitude is the secret to quality service.

Many new employees adopt an attitude that says, "Don't take advantage of me just because I am the new employee around here." Starting out with a resentful chip on your shoulder hurts your chances of building positive relationships with your fellow employees. But there's a balance. Others might take the approach of trying so hard to win approval from coworkers that they risk getting labeled as pests.

Think of yourself as an entrepreneur rather than as an employee. Perceive your organization as your market and see your manager as a customer or client. Seek out and anticipate his or her unmet needs. Often, your manager is juggling many balls in the air at one time, experiencing stress in the process. In such situations, he or she does not think of everything needed. Place yourself in your manager's position, and proactively handle what would assist him or her.

Having a genuine spirit of being of service to customers, your manager, and fellow workers, and being sincerely willing to assist them, will be noticed and appreciated. When you do a little extra for an external or internal customer, you help to retain their business (and therefore your job!). Often customers will report their satisfaction to a manager as well, which will help you at your next performance appraisal.

2. *Be open to learning:* As mentioned earlier, organizations are looking for and promoting lifetime learners. It is critically important that you have an open mind and attitude about learning new things. One of the best assets you can have for being an excellent employee and improving your chances for raises and promotions is increasing your knowledge.

As often as possible, attend training workshops. If your organization offers tuition reimbursements at a local college, sign up for classes. Attend all training workshops and seminars offered both within and outside your place of work. Read industry-related publications to stay up-to-date on current trends. Get a mentor or ask your manager to spend time explaining the business to you. Most will be flattered to be asked, pleased to share their knowledge, and happy that you are interested. Moreover, the knowledge you gain from these encounters will enable you to contribute in decision-making meetings and influence the direction of projects.

You can also build relationships by volunteering for extra activities at your workplace. Does a Toastmasters group to coach people on public-speaking skills need to be organized? Is someone needed to serve on the communications committee or other committees? Just a note of caution—do not be so involved in these activities that you seriously neglect your work or earn the resentment of coworkers who end up covering for you. If your activities are moderate, they can enable you to be better balanced.

All of these efforts on your part demonstrate to your managers that you are a motivated person who is committed to self-improvement and that you are willing to go beyond basic requirements to do more for the company. Greater knowledge, skills, and experience are assets you may bring to another company at some point as well.

3. *Be respectful:* Do your actions portray respect? Showing respect can often be as simple as remembering to return a stapler borrowed from a coworker. Sometimes it can be talking politely to another employee you meet in the hallway, or keeping your direct manager informed about your interaction with a manager in another department.

Language, too, is important. Often we portray our ignorance by the slang or poor grammar we use. Keep a dictionary nearby; try to learn one new word each day and use it in a sentence. You will be surprised how often you find yourself using it in the following weeks. This will enhance your creative and innovative skills as well.

4. *Be positive:* Be aware of how positive you are. Notice how often you complain or talk with a complaining tone of voice. Being negative and complaining keeps you stuck in the present. Being positive and addressing issues constructively allow you to move forward in life toward success.

Do not let failures dash your hopes. See them as learning experiences and move on. Abraham Lincoln experienced eight losses before he was elected president. When you have a tough break, ask yourself, "What can I learn from this? How can I be better prepared in the future?"

Realize that your future is in your hands. It does not depend on others. As playwright S. N. Behrman said, "At the end of every road you meet yourself." Hence, the key is having a positive attitude that leads to proactive behavior. Organizations seek employees who have "fire in the belly"—which means they do not stand around waiting to be told what to do. Rather they look for opportunities to do more than what is expected and then initiate such actions. Seeing the world from a positive perspective is the powerhouse behind these behaviors.

5. *Value diversity:* Organizations are coming to realize that "difference" is a valuable quality for creativity and business success. If everyone thought and acted alike, not only would new ideas slowly disappear but creative suggestions that surface would be quickly shot down. "That will never work!" or "Where did you get that crazy idea?" punctuate the workplace. Expressions such as these assume that coworkers with different ideas had better not speak up.

The population of the United States and the world is rapidly changing, and so is its workforce, which is today less dominated by white males. African-Americans, Hispanics, Asians, and many others are now commonplace in the workforce. Women are more numerous in companies, and more are achieving positions at the highest level of responsibility.

Organizations that are aware of these population trends also realize that customers often seek out members of their own ethnic or racial group because they share a common language, and they perceive a greater level of trust. Hence, hiring people of a variety of races, genders, ages, and backgrounds is an excellent strategy for attracting new customers as well as ensuring repeat business.

In addition, every worker has different strengths. Some are very meticulous and detail-oriented; others are more flexible. Both can be valuable contributors in the workplace. Learning to accept the differences of others and utilizing their strengths can make the difference between success and failure.

Janiece Greenley was hired to assist a sales manager for a busy manufacturing plant. The sales representatives started calling her and asking her to contact customers about routine requests, which helped them reduce their workload. This was not part of Janiece's original job description, so she could have refused. She said yes, however, and discovered that she was able to get to know customers, often help them with other concerns, and learn more about the plant's product line. In a few months, a sales representative position came open. Guess who was first in line to be considered for the promotion?

In the cafeteria, George Mason's white male coworkers were complaining. They criticized the company for hiring new employees with different racial and ethnic backgrounds. George was concerned that this prejudice would hurt both his white coworkers and the new employees. He spoke up and shared his own positive experiences with and observations of workplace diversity. He told a story about the creativity that happened in his last company because his team had diverse perspectives. Some of his listeners agreed to give the new employees a chance.

Be Aware of Your Behavior

1. *Take responsibility for yourself:* Be aware of your actions and their impact on others. Keep the slate clean by recognizing mistakes, admitting them, and apologizing and adjusting your behavior as needed. When you are new on the job, do not try so hard at the beginning to impress everyone with how wonderful you are. If you try to shine too fast, you may offend someone or management may set higher expectations than you can meet. Your addition to a team of people causes all of them to make adjustments. Get to know people gradually, and let them do the same with you.

2. *Be responsible, empowering, and cooperative:* Organizations are stifled by people who are overly dependent rather than responsible, intensely controlling rather than empowering, and extremely competitive rather than cooperative within the organization. To ensure your own success and the success of the enterprise, compete with your competitor, and cooperate with your associates.

Being responsible and self-empowered can include holding yourself accountable for mistakes and consequences and honestly admitting them. It means being fully involved in resolving challenges, rather than pointing fingers of blame at others. Successful employees behave as if the business is their own and act accordingly.

Every member of the organization has a responsibility to promote team communication and unified functioning. Professional jealousy, jockeying for position, and power plays leave the organization weaker and less effective. Rather, publicly complimenting those who do a good job on a specific project increases further productive behaviors by such individuals and by those who hear your words. But your compliments need to be sincere. If they seem phony, mistrust develops.

If you become aware of information that would be helpful to coworkers, make copies and share it. Make a note of occasions to celebrate, such as birthdays, new babies, or graduations, and make them happy occasions. If people are going through a difficult time, try to assist them with their work. Everything that promotes a group's smooth functioning helps the company be successful and makes it easier to have a positive work environment.

3. *Be trusting and trustful:* Many times in our culture people expect others to earn their trust before they are willing to trust. If this is common at work, the organizational climate reeks with fear and suspicion. While sometimes you can be disappointed, it is effective to go ahead and trust others until they prove untrustworthy. Moreover, your trustful actions build a bond of trust with others. Dependability is a good example. This means showing up on time for meetings and completing work by agreed-upon deadlines. Present your trust as a gift; it will be a pleasant surprise to experience trust leading to trust. It takes at least one to get the ball rolling, but in the end it results in a trusting organization.

It is most important for you not to betray another person's trust, especially confidentiality. Often coworkers share personal information, or you might accidentally hear something in an open-walled office. Once you have disappointed someone by breaking confidentiality, failing to keep promises, or becoming known as a person who gossips and backbites, regaining that trust will be very difficult. Associates will hesitate to share information with you again.

Miguel listened to Jack discuss how their coworker Jaytha insulted and embarrassed a customer. Miguel then added a comment of his own agreeing and reinforcing Jack's observation that Jaytha was not capable of doing the job. Afterward, Miguel reflected on their conversation and wondered to himself what Jack says about him when he (Miguel) is not present. Backbiting hurts everyone involved. Complaining to someone who can't do anything about the problem creates negativity.

4. *Be flexible, fast, and efficient:* The pace of change in organizations and the world is rapid and constant. Successful employees are able to adjust to changes without constant complaints. Very successful employees anticipate the changes and proactively respond to them. Part of this flexibility is the ability to accept and tolerate ambiguity and uncertainty, two things that usually accompany constant change. Employees who become very stressed-out from these conditions cannot do their best work on behalf of the company.

Most companies are conscious of the need to contain costs, so they have seen the financial value in getting tasks completed faster and more efficiently. The more you stay aware of your job and make suggestions and implement actions that promote efficiency, the more you will be valued as an employee.

5. *Think and communicate dynamically:* The days of being a passive, do-what-you-are-told employee are probably gone forever. Employers are valuing employees who can remember key company information, analyze problems, be innovative in resolving them, and make important decisions.

Communication skills are critical to being effective in working with others and consolidating relationships with customers. In addition to having some skills in writing, successful employees need to be able to make creative presentations, actively listen to others, clarify and summarize messages, give constructive feedback, and be open to receive feedback and coaching. Openness to feedback and coaching both rank high in performance appraisals.

6. *Avoid sexual harassment:* **Sexual harassment** is behavior that calls attention to gender, sexuality, or the sexual identity of people in a manner that creates a hostile environment or prevents or impairs their full enjoyment of occupational benefits or opportunities. What is often at issue is not sexual attention in itself but intimidation, coercion, or abuse of power. This behavior is especially harmful in situations where the imposition of unwanted sexual attention is accompanied by the promise of employment rewards or the threat of reprisal. It is not always clear what words or behavior qualify as harassment, however, so it is in your self-interest, as an employee, to be overly conservative. A story or joke may appear funny to one person but perceived as offensive by another. What was meant to be a touch or hug of thoughtfulness and consideration may be misunderstood as sexual harassment. So, be sure to know your audience and be clear about your intentions. At the same time, watch to make sure that you are not being overly sensitive.

7. *Act ethically and honestly:* Business ethics are guidelines that need to permeate your work. They include being honest in your written financial reports to your managers and stockholders instead of hiding information or adjusting it falsely. Ethical treatment of customers requires treating them with respect, keeping promises, and quoting fees fairly. A company that behaves ethically toward its employees does not make false promises, pays them fairly, and provides opportunities for them to be successful. Employees are often the ones who affect how a company treats the environment—recycling, handling products safely, and not polluting are all ethical behaviors. Ethical actions keep you and your company healthy and strong in the long run. If you have questions about ethics, many companies have telephone hotlines, Websites, or **ombudsman**—a confidential and neutral person to talk to.

There may be other norms that you identify throughout your work life that will contribute to your success. The more you use them the more likely it is that you will be a valued employee.

■ TIPS FOR SUCCESS ■
At Work

1. Read professional journals and business magazines.
2. Join professional and community organizations.
3. Participate in education/training programs.
4. Become clear about your career goals, and share these goals with upper management; together design an action plan for your career development and move to implement the plan.
5. Dress for the job you want to get, not the job you have.
6. Go out of your way to help at least one other employee each day.
7. Evaluate your actions and the actions of your company managers and executives to monitor if they are ethical. Seek guidance if you have concerns.
8. Maintain a positive attitude.
9. Communicate in ways that make a positive difference.

SCENARIO FOR SUCCESS

Trinh Nan Yu is in a position as a customer service specialist and sales associate trainee for Oil America, Inc., a petrochemical company specializing in small quantities of a variety of different products. He is unfamiliar with the wide range of products and with all of his company's competitors. He researches the trade magazines that apply to this field and arranges for a subscription of each to be delivered to him. As he begins to become familiar with the content of the magazines, he realizes that he can highlight and flag certain sections and share them with his peers.

Yu also begins to notice that while the information in the magazines is helpful for the sales associates with whom he is training, their busy schedules prevent them from reading as much as they need to read. He begins to share key stories with them. In addition, he outlines and summarizes salient articles, saving them time and assisting them in their jobs. His increase in knowledge and helpful actions enable him to move faster into a full-time position as a sales associate. His focus is on helping the other members of the organization as he helps himself.

Questions for Discussion
1. What actions enabled Trinh Nan Yu to succeed in his job and be promoted?
2. What tips for success have you found particularly helpful in the workplace? Why do you think they have worked well?
3. What implicit organizational norms, in retrospect, would have been beneficial for you to know in your workplace? (If you haven't been in a workplace, think of some other new organization or college class in which you participated.)

ACTIVITIES FOR SUCCESS

Activity 1: Becoming Aware of Organizational Norms

Understanding what various norms look like will assist you in following them.

Objective: Become skilled at identifying all types of norms.
Procedure: Small group discussion.
Step 1: Give examples of pivotal, relevant, and peripheral norms within your workplaces or organizations.
Step 2: List examples of pivotal, relevant, and peripheral norms in your classroom.
Step 3: List examples of pivotal, relevant, and peripheral norms within your college.
Step 4: Discuss the implications of these norms for both your success at work and in college.

Activity 2: The Smile Experiment

This experiment calls for interacting with people in a variety of ways and noting their responses to how you treat them. The experiment works best when you meet these strangers at work or at school and when they are walking alone and, therefore, not distracted by a companion.

Objectives: (1) To be aware of your own actions and behaviors; (2) to be aware of the impact of your actions and behaviors on others.
Procedure: *Note:* You might find it helpful to set up a chart or spreadsheet to track your data. A sample is provided below.
Step 1: After attaining eye contact, smile without speaking to ten strangers and note their reactions.
Step 2: After attaining eye contact, smile and say "Hello" or "Hi" (not "How are you?") to ten strangers and note their reactions.
Step 3: After attaining eye contact, frown or hold a straight face at ten strangers and note their reactions.

Smile Experiment Chart

Encounter	Smile	Individual's Response	Other Notes
1	Yes		
2	Yes		
3	Yes		
4	Yes		
5	Yes		
6	Yes		
7	Yes		
8	Yes		
9	Yes		
10	Yes		
11	Yes + hello		
12	Yes + hello		
13	Yes + hello		
14	Yes + hello		
15	Yes + hello		
16	Yes + hello		
17	Yes + hello		
18	Yes + hello		
19	Yes + hello		
20	Yes + hello		
21	Frown/stare		
22	Frown/stare		

(Continued next page)

Encounter	Smile	Individual's Response	Other Notes
23	Frown/stare		
24	Frown/stare		
25	Frown/stare		
26	Frown/stare		
27	Frown/stare		
28	Frown/stare		
29	Frown/stare		
30	Frown/stare		

Step 4: Answer the following questions:

1. What did you learn about yourself from this experiment?
2. What did you learn about others from this experiment?
3. What are the implications for your being successful in school and at work?

Activity 3: Customer Service

The quality of your service to others directly affects the quality of your work life, performance, and company success.

Objectives: (1) To assess your ability to deliver excellent customer service; (2) to set customer service improvement goals.

Procedure:

Step 1: Identify a customer (internal or external) in your work. Interview the person to determine whether or not you are meeting the needs of the person's department or company. Write down their needs and how well or poorly you are meeting them.

Step 2: Choose one need you are not currently meeting well. To meet that need, set SMARTER objectives (see Chapter 10, page 65).

JOURNAL FOR SUCCESS

Journal Entry

Objective: To reflect upon past efforts and future activities for being successful in college or at work.

Procedure: In your journal, respond to the following questions:

1. In retrospect, what norms, had you been aware of them, would have been helpful to you in previous work or school experiences? How would greater awareness have contributed to your success?
2. Having studied this chapter, what could you do differently in the future to improve the likelihood of success in college or on the job?
3. What changes in your attitudes might enable you to improve your behaviors and achieve college or occupational success?

CHAPTER 15
Life Success

If I had my life to live over again, I would have made it a rule to read some poetry and listen to some music at least once a week; for perhaps the parts of my brain now atrophied would have thus been kept active through use. The loss of these tastes is a loss of happiness, and may possibly be injurious to the intellect, and more probably to the moral character, by enfeebling the emotional part of our nature.

— Charles Darwin

To Learn and Understand

- What are the key components of a balanced life?
- What are the roles of values and goals in achieving successful balance?
- How can you tell when you are out of balance?
- How can you re-gain balance when it is lost?

15.1 INTERNAL BALANCE

You probably learned how to ride a bicycle as a child. It took try after try to understand how to hold your body, determine the best speed, and realize just how difficult the concept of balance is. You faltered or fell again and again. After persevering, however, one day everything clicked into place, and you stayed on and rode. For the rest of your life, you will now know how to achieve balance on a bicycle.

The same process holds true with achieving balance in your life. It takes time to understand your values, experiment with allocating your time, explore the areas to include in your life, and determine your life goals. As you sort through all of these, your life will increase in balance and effectiveness, culminating in success. Part of that success comes from understanding that balance consists of both internal and external components that need your care and attention.

You look after your internal balance by taking care of your physical, emotional, mental, and spiritual needs.

Physical/Emotional Needs

Taking care of your physical needs ensures that your body is available to show up for activities, and effectively participate in them. Here are some areas to pay attention to:

Diet and Exercise Exercising and eating a balanced nutritional diet helps your body ward off illnesses and maximizes your energy for study, work, and play. When you are on the go a lot with classes, work, family, and so on, diet and exercise can slip to the bottom of your priority list. You may need to be creative about finding a place for these important needs. Ride your bike to class. Use the stairs instead of the elevator when you are going up or down only a floor or two. Carry nuts, water, and a piece of fruit with you. Make sure you are calmly sitting at a table for at least one meal a day. Fit in a quick swim or a brisk walk during your lunch hour. Eating well and exercising both contribute to keeping your energy level up.

Sleep It is almost impossible to feel balance in your life if you are physically deprived of sleep. Most people can lose sleep occasionally, but repeated loss begins to have an impact on all other areas of your life. Generally, seven to eight hours of restful sleep per night is needed to avoid the negative effects of too little sleep.

Energy Work Current health research is looking at ancient healing practices that address the flow of energy throughout the body. Many people are involved in practices like Tai Chi, acupressure, or massage to harmonize their energy flows.

Feelings Feelings are good in themselves. They are part of what it means to be human. Think about how boring life would be without them. Having appropriate feelings is a sign that you are in balance. If a tragedy occurs in your life—for example, the untimely death of a loved one—and you can experience a deep sense of sadness, this is a sign that you are emotionally balanced. Similarly, if in the presence of a gorgeous sunset you can pause and deeply appreciate it, it is evidence that you are emotionally balanced.

The HALT Warning Signs HALT is an acronym formed by the words **H**ungry, **A**ngry, **L**onely, or **T**ired. These are warning signs from your body and mind that something is out of balance. If even one is a problem, you will not handle the key areas of your life very well. What is essentially important is staying aware of emotions as they occur and taking steps to work through them or express them appropriately. So, pay attention to what your body and mind are telling you.

Depression One sign that the emotional component is out of balance is when you experience "the blahs." Nothing is wrong, but nothing seems right either. You experience a lack of excitement and enthusiasm. Life seems boring. When you are in balance, the opposite is happening—you are quite aware of feelings of excitement, enthusiasm, and creativity. If the former is happening, however, you may be experiencing mild depression, and seeing a counselor at college or a therapist privately might be wise. If depression is deeper, and especially if you are experiencing suicidal thoughts, professional assistance is critical and perhaps immediately needed.

Sex Sex is a normal and natural part of life. Some people choose to abstain from sex as a part of their healthy functioning. Others choose to have sex as part of their well-being. It's important to understand your values in relation to sex and act according to them in order to stay in balance. If you go against your values in order to go along with the crowd or a particular person, you may find that the stress of the internal conflict causes physical disability and emotional pain. When your mind and actions are out of balance, you experience what is called **cognitive dissonance.** Over time, unless this incongruity is attended to, your body will likely suffer. Some people get ulcers, for example, not from what they eat but from what is eating them. Excessive guilt, remorse, and tension can be destructive to your balance and well-being.

Drugs and Alcohol You may find drugs and alcohol tempting as a means of escaping from your life or perceive them as a way to have fun. It takes very little use of either of these, however, to start experiencing negative consequences. You might get up late for class, miss a work appointment, fight with a close friend or relative, forget something important you did while under the influence, act in a way that you wouldn't otherwise, and more. It is certainly difficult to experience full success in your life if you are using these substances immoderately or illegally. There can also be a negative impact on your health.

Mental/Expressive Needs

Learning is a lifelong activity. Setting a goal to learn something new each day can bring vitality into your life. Finding ways to stimulate your mental capacity can be a significant and enriching part of your life. This might include being part of a debate club, visiting local museums, or participating in discussion groups.

Recognizing and nurturing your creativity and connections to the arts can also be a very enriching part of your life. This can include many activities such as taking a painting, weaving, or photography class; visiting an art museum; knitting; drawing; going to movies, plays, or concerts; and reading or writing poetry.

Spiritual Needs

There is a growing recognition in the world about the value of understanding and practicing some form of spirituality. Although in the past spirituality has usually been associated with organized religion, there is not necessarily such a connection. Basically, spirituality is a spiritual quest for meaning to one's life. For many people, this can be as simple as establishing a regular connection with nature. For others it can be participating in a religion, experiencing the power of prayer and a connection with God. One sign that this spiritual component is in balance is a sense of aliveness. Another is a calm centering that can occur with meditation, an excellent tool to find balance in your life.

15.2 EXTERNAL BALANCE

Taking care of your internal balance involves connecting to activities outside of yourself. These external activities provide feedback and information that in turn enable you to reevaluate and maintain your internal personal balance. The key components of external balance are family, friendships, spiritual community, work/profession, volunteer activities, and civic involvement.

At times, the balance might shift to allow for extra time in one area. Starting a new job may require extra time during the learning period. When you have a new baby, family becomes a higher priority. Over time, however, all areas need to receive balanced attention. Committing time and attention to each of these is part of being a whole human being.

Family

One of the most difficult areas to find harmony and balance is in your family. Preventing and resolving conflicts within the family is often key to feeling in balance in the rest of your life. For young adults, constant fights, disagreements, and lack of communication with parents or siblings can cause stress and imbalance. Looking to your parents solely as a source of money and not maintaining a relationship with them can cause them to feel resentful over time. For older, married adults with families, stress can build with the constant pressure of trying to keep up with everyone's busy schedules. One way to prevent conflict is to structure quality time with your family regularly. Set goals to have dinner together, play games, or go out together. Family vacations are also valuable times for developing balance. For families with serious problems, professional counseling or support groups can assist in improving communication.

Often people experience a conflict between spending time at work and time with family members. It is tempting to justify time at work by thinking, "I'm really doing this for my spouse and children." No amount of money, however, substitutes for time nurturing a marriage or children. Serious family breakdowns can occur if this imbalance becomes extreme or chronic.

Friendships

Friendships can bring happiness to your life and provide opportunities to express your concerns and feelings and to have fun. Interacting with friends often gives you insights into better ways to interact with family members. If you make a goal to structure time with a friend each day, such as making a phone call or sending an e-mail or a card, you will celebrate maintaining balance in this portion of your life.

On the other hand, one of the challenges of college life is a temptation to spend all of your non-classroom time with friends. This can interfere with completing homework assignments. Balance is the key in making your choices.

Spiritual Community

There are many options for connecting with a spiritual community. Many people choose a traditional place of worship, others investigate a new religion. People also find spiritual connections in 12-step support groups, weekend retreats, meditation groups, nature hikes, and other goal-oriented groups. You need to determine for yourself what meets your needs best. Often a spiritual group will design and fulfill community outreach projects together, fulfilling another area of balance in your life.

Career/Profession

For most people, their sense of responsibility when it comes to their career is based on their cultural upbringing. They were taught to be dependable, courteous, on time, neat, and develop other traits that are valued by employers. A career, as opposed to just "a job," gives purpose and meaning to your life, positively impacting your motivation. Doing work that you find makes a difference in other people's lives, besides providing an income, gives balance to your life. Having thoughts of anticipation and feelings of joy when you think about work activities is a sign of this balance.

The workplace is often full of opportunities to let integrity slip. Sometimes it is tempting to lie to a manager about work not done, make a promise to a customer you cannot keep, or cheat on an expense account. Operating in this way, however, sets up an internal conflict that interferes with feeling whole and balanced in your life.

Before pursuing an opportunity at work that has new or increased responsibilities, it is beneficial to understand your values and the impact of the position on your life. Do you need the salary increase? Will it mean more time away from family? Will it give you skills that you can apply in other areas of your life? Will it enable you to be of greater service to more people? Would you be comfortable with your children knowing what you are doing?

In evaluating balance in your current position, it is effective to begin by evaluating your needs and how you meet them. Do you need to ask for assistance with workload? Would having a cellular/mobile phone or PDA help or hurt? Can you delegate some of your tasks? Are you hanging on to activities that you could delegate because you like doing them or believe no one can do them as well as you can? Do you need to train a backup person to cover work in your absence so you aren't overwhelmed upon your return? Are you communicating your needs to your manager? Are you setting limits on interruptions? Do you need time for management training? Once this evaluation is complete, you can begin to negotiate with your coworkers and managers to have your needs met.

Experts are starting to recognize that enjoying yourself at work, even having fun, is possible and increases commitment and productivity. Look for points of humor and cultivate relationships that are open to laughter. Author Norman Cousins in *Anatomy of an Illness As Perceived by the Patient,* demonstrates that laughter releases one's endorphins (hormones that promote a positive mood) and strengthens one's immune system. The more you laugh, the healthier you become.

Making a commitment to take advantage of learning and training opportunities at work broadens your knowledge and skill base and increases your value as an employee. Look for opportunities to learn what others know and do on their jobs. Make a goal to volunteer to help them out regularly. Tell yourself you can find time if this assisting is a high priority for you. Growing and developing as an employee is often a key to being fulfilled in your work life, which helps you maintain balance.

Managing Money

Managing money effectively is a skill most people struggle with during their lives. Preoccupation with financial problems in particular can cause people a high level of stress and make it difficult to be involved in other areas of life. Juggling college and work and at the same time keeping up with expenses often leads students to get behind financially. Overuse of credit cards, which might seem like "free money" to first-time users, compounds the problem when bills and high interest rates become unmanageable. You may also incur student loans as debts that will have to be paid back when you are out of college. Be cautious and use the loan money for school-related matters like tuition and books rather than for personal expenses. Many agencies, classes, and individuals can assist people to learn money-management skills such as budgeting and balancing a checkbook, and credit-counseling services are available. If money matters are causing you problems, it is important to seek help. It is better to learn the skills as soon as possible before your money issues become overwhelming.

Volunteer Involvement

Most nonprofit agencies in North America cannot survive without volunteers. People who volunteer can see the difference their efforts make on the lives of others. Outreach to others without expecting anything in return is often difficult to practice, but it is an important part of your learning. You usually end up receiving far more than you give because personal learning, growth, and gratitude often come back to you.

Structure specific activities into your life that will ensure this balance. This might be as simple as helping an elderly neighbor by putting the garbage out each week for pickup. You might volunteer to teach children to read, or you might become a big sister or big brother to a child lacking a parent. Some people have found meaning by opening their homes to exchange students from other countries. You will be amazed at how much meaning and feelings of significance enter your life when you embark upon such a journey toward balance.

Civic Involvement

Local governments often operate effectively because people seriously care about city services, school quality, and community activities. People can find it very rewarding to serve on city councils, zoning commissions, community councils, school boards, and other civic groups. Others may find their balance by being less involved, but taking time to learn about issues and voting responsibly. Still others might join an environmental organization and work on campaigns to resolve pollution issues. What is important is understanding that part of being balanced as a human being is caring about the structure and environment around you and doing your part to keep it functioning well.

■ TIPS FOR SUCCESS ■
In Life

1. Drink plenty of water every day.
2. Do aerobic exercise for at least twenty minutes at least three times a week.
3. Connect with one person you really care about every day.
4. Each day make an effort to thank someone by writing a note, making a phone call, sending an e-mail, or expressing your gratitude in person.
5. Smile at people you meet and cheerfully greet them.
6. Go for a walk or stop at a park on your way home from work or classes each day to collect your thoughts and get in touch with what you are feeling.
7. Listen more than you talk.
8. Ask for help with a task so others can experience the joy of giving.
9. Take a daily personal inventory of your actions and attitudes and clean up issues as they come up.
10. Connect with at least one current customer every day to express your gratitude for their business.
11. Don't blame others for problems; ask "What can we do to resolve this?"
12. Don't spend beyond your income.

SCENARIO FOR SUCCESS

Brigit Drewar is a volunteer coordinator for Cherish Center, a hospice specializing in care of terminal cancer patients. Although she is in a salaried position, the 120 volunteers she manages receive no compensation. Once a year, she plans a volunteer appreciation dinner and gives a plaque to the volunteer with the most volunteer hours. She works with local businesses to obtain discount coupons for all volunteers, and she obtains complimentary tickets to amusement parks and entertainment events that go to the "volunteer of the week." When she notices a volunteer being especially caring to a family, she writes them a special note of appreciation. She regularly circulates among the volunteers, giving compliments as she goes. While other agencies in the area have declining volunteer enrollment, Brigit has no trouble maintaining hers.

Questions for Discussion

1. What volunteer activities are you presently engaged in?
2. What volunteering behaviors on the part of your parents led you to volunteer early in your life?
3. In what way can you see yourself voluntarily contributing to the success of your college community or your neighborhood?
4. How might volunteering contribute to your academic and career growth?

ACTIVITIES FOR SUCCESS

Activity 1: Becoming Aware of Imbalance

The constant work of maintaining balance in your life requires a high degree of self-awareness.

Objectives: (1) To identify your current activities; (2) to identify places that are out of balance; (3) to set goals to establish or restore balance.

Procedure:

Step 1: Give examples of activities with which you are currently involved in the following areas:

1. Personal
2. Social
3. Professional
4. Community

Step 2: List examples of activities you could do in these areas to bring balance in your life:

1. Personal
2. Social
3. Professional
4. Community

Step 3: Set SMARTER goals to find balance. (For an explanation of these goals, see Chapter 10, page 65.)

Activity 2: Experiment in Finding Personal Balance

Sometimes spending time alone can support reducing stress and restoring balance.

Objectives: (1) Experience a quiet space; (2) assess the experience of being in a quiet space.

Procedure:

Step 1: Find a quiet place such as a wooded area with a stream or a lake. Spend thirty to sixty minutes there alone with the intent of doing nothing. Pay attention to your breathing. Breathe in relaxation and breathe out discouragement, depression, and bitterness. Focus only upon what is happening in the present. Receive the present as truly a gift. Note what you are thinking and especially feeling. If memories from the past or thoughts of all the things you need to do in the future interrupt your awareness of the present, do not become disturbed by the distraction. Simply say "next" to yourself, as if you were turning a page of a book, and gently bring yourself back to the present.

Step 2: Do you see any benefit in incorporating regular periods of quiet meditation like this into your life to promote balance? If so, set a SMARTER goal to achieve this benefit. (For an explanation of these goals, see Chapter 10, page 65.)

JOURNAL FOR SUCCESS

Journal Entry

Our lives are so loaded with distractions. We need to find some time simply to be aware or life will pass us by with limited joy.

Objective: To develop greater and greater awareness of the present.

Procedure: After completing Activity 2, write what you have learned from this experience. These reflective questions may assist you in what to look for:

1. What thoughts and feelings did you experience in the present?
2. Were you successful at bringing yourself back to the present? Did you find any other method that was helpful?
3. Did you notice a change in your state of mind or level of energy between the beginning and the end of the activity?
4. What insights did you gain about yourself as you focused on the present in a natural environment?

BIBLIOGRAPHY

Bloom, Benjamin. *Taxonomy of Educational Objectives*. New York: David McKay, 1956.

Burns, John. *Feeling Good*. New York: Morrow, 1989.

Callahan, Betsy N. *Assertiveness Training*. Boston: Resource Communications, 1980.

Capacchione, Lucia. *The Power of Your Other Hand*. North Hollywood, CA: Newcastle Publishing, 1988.

Chopra, Deepak. *Ageless Body, Timeless Mind*. New York: Harmony Books, 1993.

Dawson, Peter. *Fundamentals of Organizational Behavior*. Englewood Cliffs, NJ: Prentice Hall, 1985.

Farnhan, Alan, and Joyce E. Davis. "How to Nurture Creative Sparks." *Fortune,* January 1994, 94.

Griffiths, Gary, Computer Instructor, Polaris Center, Cleveland, OH. Personal interview. September 2002.

Heidersbach, Annie. Director of Career Services, Baldwin-Wallace College, Berea, OH. Personal interview, October 2001.

Hoovler, Karen S. Career Consultant/School Psychologist, Baldwin-Wallace College, Berea, OH. Personal interview, October 2001.

Idea Connections. *Ten Principles for Creating Synergy*. Rochester, NY: Idea Connections, Inc., 1989.

Orioli, Esther. *The Stress Map*. San Francisco: Essi Systems, 1991.

Pauk, Walter. *How to Study in College*. Boston: Houghton Mifflin, 2001.

Linda Kavelin Popov. The Virtues Project 35Y Educator's Guide. Torrance, CA: Jalmar Press, 2000.

Rosenberg, Marshall B. *Nonviolent Communication: A Language of Compassion*. DelMar, CA: PuddleDancer Press, 1999.

Samovar, Leroy A., and Richard E. Porter. *Intercultural Communication*. Belmont, CA: Wadsworth, 1991.

Schein, Edgar H.. "Organizational Socialization." In *Organizational Psychology: Readings on Human Behavior in Organizations*, edited by David A. Kolb, Irwin M. Rubin, and James M. McIntyre. Englewood Cliffs, NJ: Prentice Hall, 1984.

Schuster, Martin, and Werner Metzig. *Learning to Learn*. Heidelberg, Germany: Springer Verlag, 1993.

Terkel, Studs. *Working*. New York: Pantheon, 1974.

Tice, Louis. *Visualization*. Seattle: Pacific Institute, 1980.

Toastmasters International. "Tips for Successful Public Speaking." Accessed online at www.toastmasters.org/tips.asp.

von Oech, Roger. *A Whack on the Side of the Head*. New York: Warner Books, 1983.

Wall, Steve, and Harvey Arden. *Wisdomkeepers*. Hillsboro, OR: Beyond Words Publishing, 1990.

STUDENT QUESTIONNAIRE

TO THE READER:

We hope that this textbook has provided you with some direction on your road to success. We would like to receive any feedback that you may have regarding the material presented on these pages. Your input would be greatly appreciated!

—The Authors

Directions: Please complete the following statements. You may use another sheet of paper if necessary.

1. I did/did not [circle one] like this textbook overall for the following reasons:

2. The most helpful part/section of this textbook was [explain why]:

3. The least helpful part/section of this textbook was [explain why]:

4. If I were the author, I would change the textbook in the following way(s):

5. If I were a professor/manager, I would/would not [circle one] change the textbook for the following reasons:

6. Do you have any additional comments/suggestions?

When you have completed this questionnaire, please mail it to

Professor Harry J. Bury
Baldwin-Wallace College
275 Eastland Road
Berea, OH 44017
Or you can e-mail it to him at < **hbury@bw.edu** >.